John Neugebauer &
Jane Evans-Brain

EMPLOYABILITY

Making the Most of Your Career Development

Los Angeles | London | New Delhi
Singapore | Washington DC | Melbourne

Los Angeles | London | New Delhi
Singapore | Washington DC | Melbourne

SAGE Publications Ltd
1 Oliver's Yard
55 City Road
London EC1Y 1SP

SAGE Publications Inc.
2455 Teller Road
Thousand Oaks, California 91320

SAGE Publications India Pvt Ltd
B 1/I 1 Mohan Cooperative Industrial Area
Mathura Road
New Delhi 110 044

SAGE Publications Asia-Pacific Pte Ltd
3 Church Street
#10-04 Samsung Hub
Singapore 049483

Editor: Matthew Waters
Editorial assistant: Lyndsay Aitken
Production editor: Sarah Cooke
Copyeditor: Solveig Gardner Servian
Proofreader: Tom Hickman
Indexer: Judith Lavender
Marketing manager: Catherine Slinn
Cover design: Francis Kenney
Typeset by: C&M Digitals (P) Ltd, Chennai, India
Printed and bound by CPI Group (UK) Ltd,
Croydon, CR0 4YY

Library of Congress Control Number: 2015959295

British Library Cataloguing in Publication data

A catalogue record for this book is available from
the British Library

ISBN 978–1-44629–834–3
ISBN 978–1-44629–835–0 (pbk)

At SAGE we take sustainability seriously. Most of our products are printed in the UK using FSC papers and boards.
When we print overseas we ensure sustainable papers are used as measured by the PREPS grading system.
We undertake an annual audit to monitor our sustainability.

Dedication

For Ruth Davidson, John Neugebauer,
Sophia Davidson and Bethan Evans-Brain.

And to all those who, having worked so hard to achieve
their degrees, now embark on their career journeys.
We hope this book will help you.

Contents

About the Authors

Dr John Neugebauer FCIPD is a Visiting Research Fellow at Bristol Business School, University of the West of England. He has had international and UK experience as an HR executive and has researched managerial careers and taught with the Open University, Bath University and Bristol University. He is an external examiner at Plymouth Business School and Bristol University Dental School. Prior to his academic career, he was Head of HR for a national organisation. He is a qualified coach, and has had extensive experience working and consulting in private sector (national and international), public sector, and third-sector organisations.

Jane Evans-Brain is a human resource business partner in a large national organisation, and has over twenty-eight years HR experience in recruitment, learning in the workplace, talent development, training, employment law, assessment centres and change management. Jane also has experience of external consulting.

Acknowledgements

We record our thanks to those at organisations who discussed employment with us, including: Jane Hadfield at North Bristol NHS Trust; Patrick Goh, Head of Global HR People & Organisation Development, Tearfund; Reverend Sam Rushton, Diocesan Director of Ordinands and Adviser for the Licensed Ministry of the Church of England, Bristol Diocese; Dr Jenny Chen, Senior Lecturer in Human Resource Management; Helen Hammond of Elephant Creative for sharing her specialised experience on social media and job search; Dr Tilly Line, Senior Careers Consultant, Employability and Enterprise Team, University of the West of England; Sarah Harper, Goldman Sachs; Professor Julie McLeod, Pro Vice-Chancellor (Student Experience), Oxford Brookes University; at RHP Group in south-west London, Executive Director of Corporate Services, Amina Graham, Chloe Marsh and John C. Neugebauer; Allie Whelan, Director Leap UK; Jenny Body, first woman president of the Royal Aeronautical Society; and Brian Staines, former Head of Careers Guidance at the University of Bristol.

We also wish to thank the many people in their early careers after graduation who gave so willingly to contribute to the additional research for this book. Their data has been recorded anonymously in the book in order to preserve confidentiality. However, those who have given permission for us to acknowledge their contribution are: Aamer Chaudhry, Abdi Omar, Alex Barnes, Alison Barnard, Amber Cunnington, Andrew Piggott, Charlotte Walker, Donal Kelly, Emily Skew, Fahad Rahman, Fiona Robertson, Gareth Neugebauer, Hannah Christie, Hugh Willan, Iestyn Davies, Jo Taylor, Kate Skew, Katie Holmes, Kerry Fey, Laura Evans, Laura Riches, Mike Hindle, Mims Harrison, Owain Davies, Peter Harry, Pippa Bell, Rachel Manse, John C. Neugebauer, Rebecca Francis, Rita Kurucz, Sarah Graham, Sophie Pearn, Steffan Lewis, Stephen Taylor, Stuart Christie and Tom Skew.

Our thanks also to Matthew Waters, Commissioning Editor at SAGE, copy-editor Solveig Gardner Servian, and Molly Farrell and Lyndsay Aitken at SAGE for their patient support and guidance while this book has been prepared.

Permissions

We have sought permission to use material from other sources, and this permission is shown where appropriate.

Myers Briggs: The Myers and Briggs Foundation, www.myersbriggs.org/more-about-personality-type/permissions/

HESA statistics have been used with permission, though the HESA wishes to point out that it cannot accept responsibility for any inferences or conclusions derived from the data by third parties.

1

Introduction

About This Book

For many graduates, looking for a future career – employability – may be the ultimate goal of several years in higher education, stress, hard work and accumulation of student debt. Little wonder that it is seen as a decision to 'get right'. But finding the right career is more than that: it is about making work choices which, for many, will be the start of a journey lasting forty years or more. Indeed, for most graduating today, the cliché – which is nevertheless true – is that we will finish our career undertaking roles, or certainly ways of working, which are unknown today.

Charles Handy (1994a) discusses how difficult it is to manage, control, predict and be part of contemporary society – what some people refer to as 'being on the edge of chaos'. In a separate publication, Handy (1994b: 14) suggests that navigating a contemporary career and managing through the dynamics and paradoxes of organisational life is akin to walking in a wood on a dark night. It is eerie, confusing to the senses, even frightening, but by dawn your path and way forward become clear.

Developing your career path may be a daunting prospect but it is undoubtedly an exciting one too. With the help of this book we hope that you will feel able to meet the career challenge. And as you do so you join a large employment pool, both in the UK and globally (see ICEF, 2012).

In 2013–2014, the UK produced 777,800 graduates (HESA, 2015); of these, 258,000 were postgraduate degrees. Some degree subjects make it easier to find work (see Appendix A), with vocational training in medicine, dentistry, education and professions allied to medicine the easiest route (at least, in 2012–2013) into finding work, with unemployment rates of 1.3 per cent to 2.4 per cent. On the other hand, unemployment rates of 4 per cent to a highest rate of 11.9 per cent (for computer sciences) apply to other subjects, with 6–8 per cent being the unemployment rates experienced by most subject graduates (HESA, 2014a). The distribution of graduate destinations by industry is shown in Table 1.1.

By 2020, it is projected that 40 per cent of the world's graduates will come from China and India (ICEF Monitor, 2012). Some estimates suggest that China alone already produces over 500,000 graduate engineers a year, a number similar to the entire UK first degree annual graduate population.

Little wonder therefore that the competition for graduate roles is so intense. Somewhat dispiritingly, the UK Chartered Institute of Personnel and Development (CIPD) published research suggesting that up to 58.8 per cent of UK graduates were in roles which did not require a degree (CIPD, 2015b). Of course, CIPD is not debasing the intrinsic value of education represented in a degree. The report also notes the increasing number of jobs which do require a degree, but that competition for graduate-level jobs has also increased. Obtaining a degree requires an enormous investment in time, money and emotional resource before entering a competitive workplace. In this book we explain how to make the most of employability opportunities and reinforce the fact that the work and life opportunities from a degree (or vocational training, or any work experience) are what *you* make of them.

TABLE 1.1   Industries of higher education leavers in employment 2012/13

Industry	Number	Percentage
Education	66,560	20.4
Health and social work	64,630	19.8
Wholesale/retail trade and vehicle repair	34,380	10.5
Professional, scientific and technical	33,290	10.2
Public administration/defence/ social security	19,450	6.0
Information and communication	17,405	5.3
Hotels and restaurants	14,305	4.4
Manufacturing	14,085	4.3
Arts, entertainment and recreation	12,975	4.0
Administrative and support services	12,725	3.9
Financial activities	12,190	3.7
Construction	5,720	1.8
Other service activities	4,770	1.5
Transport and storage	3,975	1.2
Real estate	3,455	1.1
Mining and quarrying	2,185	0.7
Electricity and gas	1,480	0.5
Water supply and waste management	950	0.3
Agriculture, forestry and fishing	750	0.2
Private households with employed persons	425	0.1
International organisations and bodies	255	0.1
Unknown	1,225	

Source: Higher Education Statistics Agency (2014b) (Used with permission)

We will see that employability after graduation is not a problem for a minority of graduates in truly elite universities (the top three or four in each country), other than for the choice of options. This is because equally elite employers court them with dinners, sponsorship and work experience from their first year at university, with early job offers on graduation. But for the rest of us, employability is more of a challenge and more of a journey. This book has been written by 'the rest of us' for 'the rest of us' to help you navigate that journey – from the time you are a student until you are more established within your chosen career.

Structure of the Book

We have structured this book to give practical guidance in employability and to support studies in employability.

At the practical level, we have included our own experiences of people management and augmented this with interviewees with a selection of educationalists, careers advisers and employers.

At the academic level, university will have taught us to learn from exposure to theory, research-based evidence or word of mouth, including anecdotes and sharing experiences with friends. Each approach has an important role to play in how we develop our learning and making sense of the world around us. Many of us will have learned that 'there is nothing so practical as a good theory' (attributed by Tolman et al., 1996: 31 to Kurt Lewin). We are encouraged to look at empirical evidence, and we may also make senses of the world through word-of-mouth narratives. Therefore in addition to reviewing relevant theory in each chapter, we have used interviews with current representatives in employment and education.

The research undertaken specifically for the book is not intended to meet empirical research standards, but it is intended to bring a contemporary and practical perspective about the world of work. As the education and employer interviews have been conducted across a wide range of graduate careers, we have been struck by the similarity, not the differences, in the messages about what makes a graduate 'employable'. Furthermore, the book is written by authors with a combined experience of working in graduate and people education and management covering over 70 years.

Employer and Education Research

We wanted this book to have a reliable range of voices from academic and practitioner sources, therefore we have considered previously published research around graduate employment. We have also undertaken direct interviews with a range of employers, higher education specialists and careers specialists. We have added our own experiences of people management, recruitment, assessment, learning and development and higher education. As a result, the book combines both theoretical and practical experiences of the workplace.

Taking these sources together, we certainly do not claim that there is a single view on graduate employability. Even so, there are significant – and repeated – lessons on how graduates can be more effective in their job searches and career development. In our professional lives and having prepared the research for the book, we have tended to find – unsurprisingly – that the vast majority of graduates are, of course, 'employable'. But the mismatch is how effectively graduates themselves prepare themselves for work, and how this then impacts on their capability to show themselves as 'employable'. From being 'employable', we then look at how to make the most of employment opportunities, and some of the challenges which will be faced during working lives.

Our aim is to bring all these lessons together into a single source book and provide an informed and accessible guide on making the most of employment opportunities at graduation and beyond.

Employability is not a state that can be induced in the final months of higher education and then simply sustained. Instead, as will be reinforced in the book, good employability prospects often start with groundwork in the final years of schooling, and will certainly need further development once in organisational life. Challenging as it may be at the time of graduation, university life is/was simply one stage on a lifelong journey.

Employability Panel

In preparation for the book, we asked 50 graduates to complete a questionnaire about their experiences in finding work and developing their early careers. We call this research the 'Employability Panel'. Panel

TABLE 1.2   Employability Panel (n=50)

Age Range	Range: 21–35	Mean Average: 25.9	
Work Experience (years)	Range: 0.25–9	Mean Average: 3	
Gender	Male: 40%	Female: 60%	
Sector Experience	Public: 44%	Private: 53%	Not-for-Profit: 3%
First Degree	100%		
Postgraduate and Higher Degree	43%		
Professional Qualifications	50%		

Examples of professional roles covered:

Administrator; Aviation; Automotive Engineer; Banking; Civil Engineer; Clinical Scientist; Communication Support Worker (Deaf); Creative Product Designer; Disability Services; Fine Art; General Practice Medical Practitioner; Higher Education Administration; Hospitality; HRM; Marine Engineer; Automotive Engineer; Marketing; Musician (Freelance Orchestral); Own business; PhD Students; Project Manager/Administrator; Quantity Surveyor; Retail Design; Social Worker; Solicitor; Teacher participants' experiences covered private, public and third-sector roles. Many were in roles as part of their early careers; others were still searching for the right openings; and some were already in portfolio careers (which we examine in Chapter 2), where they combined jobs such as museum keeping, or even street cleaning, with other passions such as conservation, art or playing in top-quality orchestras. Further details of the Employability Panel are given in Table 1.2.

We do not claim that the research panel is statistically representative. Instead, the Employability Panel is used in the book to illustrate some of the lived experiences – the challenges and successes – in finding work and in developing a career in the early years until the age of 35. Throughout the book we also use statistics from recognised public sources.

Career Case Studies

Even with 50 case studies, the Employability Panel reminds us of the enormous range of graduate opportunities and the even more diverse paths to achieving them. In Appendix D, we show some representative case studies (marine engineering, clinical scientist, marketer, solicitor, teacher and social worker) of how graduates got into the roles they now hold.

Whilst each of the case studies is in a very different occupational field, they show that there are no simple and straight paths to finding the right roles for the future. In every case, the interviewee encountered periods of uncertainty and doubt about the future. Indeed, in some cases candidates took a circular, untypical route into establishing themselves in their chosen career paths; in other cases they showed great resilience and determination, even when they had not progressed through conventional career paths. However, the important thing is that, in the end, all found the career outcomes they were seeking.

The paths to achieving success were very individualistic but used the different approaches described below in 'Practical Application'. The key to success in each case was determination.

Using the Book

This book has been written predominantly for the UK job market, but many of the lessons are applicable more globally. After several years of difficulty, the UK graduate market started to improve in 2014 (Association of Graduate Careers Advisory Services, 2015). However, to underline that even applying for jobs in the UK is to apply against global competition, the UK Government announced in June 2015 that it had capped visa work applications for non-European Union (EU) skilled migrants at 20,700 for the year. The press reported that this left a wide range of roles unfilled, including in graduate training schemes in London. Whilst employer representatives claim that non-EU workers represent only 0.066 per cent of the UK labour market, these figures both underline the opportunities available for graduates as well as the levels of international competition in being successfully selected.

Our professional experience and academic research have reinforced our belief that employability is not simply about finding that first job after leaving university – important as that may be. It is about developing, finding and then making the most of opportunities, having the resilience to deal with setbacks, and having vision and determination to maintain a long-term perspective of career aims.

Therefore the book will be valuable at all stages of your student and working life:

If you are still studying, the book will help you understand the world of work and, critically, the need to start early in enquiry, experience and preparation for future work.

As you leave education, it will help you to look at the range of possible career paths and the opportunities and challenges you may expect to face.

Once you are in work, the book will help you to navigate your way through the opportunities and occasional cul-de-sacs which characterise working lives in the twenty-first century. The book has been written to prepare readers for the workplace, but will be equally valuable as a return-to-source once at work.

In this first chapter we introduce the topic of 'employability'. We summarise some of the academic perspectives on the subject, and also look at what graduates themselves, representative employers and representatives of higher education say on the subject. In our view some – though not all – of the academic research on employability, as well as the emphasis from universities themselves, focuses too much on transition from student life to working life. Therefore we conclude the chapter with our own model of employability, which includes that first job, and then goes beyond to look at successful personal development and achievement in working life.

In the second chapter we discuss careers and how the concept of career has developed and been challenged in the twenty-first century. The chapter considers the stages of career, and critically considers concepts of career such as 'boundaryless' and 'portfolio' careers. We look at whether there are generational differences in how careers and working life are approached. For those not sure what they want to do in the future, psychometric tests may be of help; we discuss these, but with the proviso that experiencing particular types of work probably counts for more than psychometric test results. The chapter concludes with an invitation to the reader to consider personal career paths.

Employability needs to be nurtured, so in Chapter 3 we look at preparations for work, including making the most of any work-related experience. Internships and placements are covered, but we also discuss how to make positive use of more casual paid and unpaid work in demonstrating your passion for your job applications. We recognise that some graduates may need additional support with their job seeking. Our Employability Panel suggested that university careers services were not strongly valued in the support which individual students received. Discussing this with careers advisers, we became convinced that part of this problem was a failure to understand how to make the best use of careers services, and we urge readers to plan and develop their interactions with their local offices. Graduates with personal disability may need additional support in finding a career role, so we signpost the facilities which can help them.

In Chapter 4 we look at finding work and navigating the labyrinth of opportunities and (for some) disappointments. We summarise some of the best practice in applications, initial sifting interviews, CVs and assessment centres. In keeping with the theme of the book, to look at both theory and practice, we explain some of the research in recruitment resourcing and how and why unconscious bias can creep into selection decisions. Early graduate work experience is often regarded as university versus work, as in two distinct stages. However, we can also look at it as part of the continuum from assessment to settling into the work, so this chapter also explores some of the early experience graduates encounter in their first 6–12 months of work, including induction in a section on 'onboarding' which has been written by our colleague Dr Jenny Chen.

Therefore in the first four chapters of the book our main focus has been on preparing for work, having a sense of future career, finding work and settling into the first job. If the employability agenda is only about the statistics of moving away from university into work or further study, that would be the finish of the book. However, real employability is about a personal commitment to continue to grow in the workplace – partly to find self-fulfilment, and partly to be sufficiently robust to make changes when desired or when needed through job restructuring. Therefore the remaining chapters take at a deeper and more sustaining look at understanding the workplace and how we adjust to its demands.

Learning is at the centre of employability. Chapter 5 considers the workplace learning agenda. We explore the roles which work organisations and professional bodies have in workplace learning and some of the current debates in training, learning and development and the most effective ways this can be undertaken. We also look at talent schemes, used by many organisations to develop key skills, management and leadership abilities for their organisations' futures. However, whilst support for your learning and development will often come from your employer, we argue that the only sure way to achieve development is through your personal ownership of your learning plan and your commitment to making it a success. We discuss learning styles and how to develop and use a learning plan; we also recommend that mentoring is an effective way to settle into your role and as a long-term support for your career.

Progress and navigation in the workplace are the themes of Chapter 6. By this time we expect that you have found a role which will make good use of your skills for the foreseeable future. Therefore, having reviewed what work means to people in the UK, we concentrate on some of the deeper challenges of work. We consider the importance of balancing work and life, and consider why diversity and inclusion remain unfinished business whether in the UK or in many international work settings. If you are considering the opportunities of international work experience, we include an overview of some of the issues you should consider. The chapter finishes with a review of how to make the most of your skills in working in teams and in dealing with change.

In Chapter 7 we look at some of the deeper issues of personal meaning in the workplace. We look at the factors which (according to research) will affect your workplace commitment. We also consider the subtleties of workplace culture, and how and why these may make your work experience positive or threaten to derail not only you but possibly the organisation within which you work. The chapter includes a discussion about emotional intelligence, self-efficacy (self-belief), workplace ethics and politics, and practical advice about how to deal with these.

To conclude the book, Chapter 8 summarises the key learning from the book. We also include our top 20 tips – not just to find work, but to be fulfilled and progressed in your chosen working lives.

Employability

Employability is for your career, not just graduation! How we manage our employability, whether at the time of graduation or throughout our working lives, requires a methodical approach to complement the investment of time and attention given to studies. Because of this, this book on the theory and practice of employability looks beyond the process of finding a job at the conclusion of higher education. Employability is a state which maintains and develops work-related skills and knowledge throughout an individual's working life.

Of course, employability depends both on demand side issues (organisations with role vacancies) as well as supply side issues (individuals' readiness to join the job market). We have concentrated on the supply side – helping you to develop and reinforce your employability skills.

Beyond the natural progression of finding work at the conclusion of studies, employability has developed into an area of interest – and often concern – for students, universities and employers. It has also become a focus of wider academic research in its own right. Later in this chapter we will explain our own employability model. Before we do so, we consider the academic perspective and research and contemporary advice from representatives of universities and graduate employers.

What Is Employability? An Academic Perspective

Employability has been defined as:

> A set of achievements – skills, understandings and personal attributes – that makes graduates more likely to gain employment and be successful in their chosen occupations, which benefits themselves, the workforce, the community and the economy. (Knight and Yorke, 2003:3)

More briefly, Rothwell and Arnold (2007: 25) defined employability as 'the ability to keep the job one has or to get the job one desires'. There is little doubt that the meaning and seriousness of 'employability' has changed over the previous 30–40 years (de Grip et al., 2004) as governments, individuals and employers respond to changes, including those in the labour market. Equally, how we see employability may reflect on our different perspectives as individuals, employers or government (Rothwell and Arnold, 2007).

Pegg et al. (2012) saw employability as comprising sound educational background, demonstrable personal and professional skills and personal attributes. However, in their review of literature on employability, Rothwell and Arnold (2007) note that there is no commonly accepted definition of employability, or, at best, that the definitions have developed over time. They cite Rajan et al.'s observation (2000: 23) that 'employability' was a word which had moved from jargon to cliché, without meaning anything in between. Even so, academic researchers acknowledge that there are two elements in employability: individual attributes and external labour market conditions. Rothwell and Arnold (2007) caution, however, that although there have been a wide range of papers written on the two elements of employability, empirical literature on employability was very limited.

In many ways the academic perspective of employability is awfully dry and dull. But we argue that employability is much bigger than this.

We have already seen that many people entering the workforce now will later be doing jobs which currently do not even exist; and a good proportion will enter graduate roles which will no longer exist in their current form. Therefore employability is about developing the skills to find work that is engaging and rewarding for the whole of our working lives. Employability is dynamic and vibrant, and in line with our personal values.

Later in this chapter we will hear what employers and universities say about graduate employability readiness. In the meantime, it is worth reviewing academic research. Raybould and Sheedy (2005) remind us that about 64 per cent of vacancies requiring graduate-level skills do not require specific degree subjects, since high levels of competency in soft skills are seen as just as important.

Employability does not solely rely on vertical progression (promotion) within the organisation. Once started on a career path, employees should consider how they would adjust to a desire – or unexpected requirement – to find a different role. Van der Heijden (2002) notes that job changes may come suddenly and without much warning, and that it is difficult to predict what professional and transferable skills may be required. She also notes the challenges and tensions in developing other areas of expertise with horizontal progression (job moves at the same grade, without promotion), even though this is to the advantage of the employee (for greater role flexibility) and the organisation (by spreading knowledge across the organisation, as well as having employees who can work in more than one area). Therefore it may seem common sense that good long-term employability will depend on being able to switch to another role. In practice the need to be seen as a specialist, and to perform in the current role, may crowd out the opportunities for developing a broad career base. Van der Heijden (2002) sees the ability to learn and transfer new skills during a career as key to longer-term employability. Therefore in Chapter 5 we concentrate on developing learning once you are in the workplace.

Employer's Perspectives

In addition to considering research that has already been published on employability, we asked a range of educational specialists, employers and employer intermediaries how they would define employability.

Employers, whether or not we may feel it is justified, are constantly complaining about the 'work readiness' of graduates. Many also complain about the shortage of 'suitable talent'. According to the Organisation for Economic Co-Operation and Development (OECD,

2015: 15), 10 per cent of new graduates have poor literacy skills and 14 per cent have poor numeracy skills. Graduates' numeracy skills in the UK are amongst the weakest of the 33 countries reviewed by the OECD. These perceptions matter because of the international mobility of labour – and so competition for roles. Furthermore, the UK is one of the few countries, according to the OECD, where graduate numeracy and literacy are judged to be lower than those of middle-aged adults (OECD 2015). The better news is that graduates in the UK appear to be stronger than those of middle age in problem solving.

Professor Julie McLeod, Pro Vice-Chancellor (Student Experience), Oxford Brookes University, commented that

> Employability is about getting into graduate-level roles, and feeling confident in furthering their future careers.

> Employability prepares people for graduate-level work and lifelong learning. (Authors' interview)

Within the UK, the Confederation of British Industry (CBI), an organisation established to represent the views of UK industry, reported in 2009 that 82 per cent of its respondents felt that universities should be 'improving employability skills [of graduates]'. They found that they were less concerned with degree and the name of the university attended (Figure 1.1).

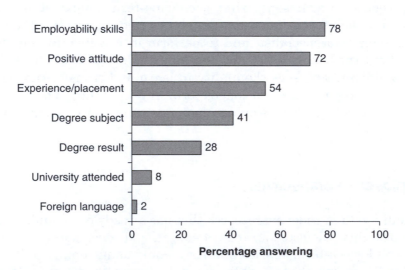

FIGURE 1.1 Important factors considered when recruiting graduates (CBI, 2009: 21, used with permission)

As to which employability skills need to be developed, the CBI identified eight core skills, and these are set out in Exhibit 1.1.

Exhibit 1.1

Employability skills – the CBI view

Employability skills include:

Self-management: readiness to accept responsibility, flexibility, resilience, self-starting, appropriate assertiveness, time management, readiness to improve own performance based on feedback/reflective learning.

Teamworking: respecting others, co-operating, negotiating/persuading, contributing to discussions, and awareness of interdependence with others.

Business and customer awareness: basic understanding of the key drivers for business success – including the importance of innovation and taking calculated risks – and the need to provide customer satisfaction and build customer loyalty.

Problem solving: analysing facts and situations and applying creative thinking to develop appropriate solutions.

Communication and literacy: application of literacy, ability to produce clear, structured written work and oral literacy – including listening and questioning.

Application of numeracy: manipulation of numbers, general mathematical awareness and its application in practical contexts (e.g. measuring, weighing, estimating and applying formulae).

Application of information technology: basic IT skills, including familiarity with word processing, spreadsheets, file management and use of internet search engines.

Entrepreneurship/enterprise: demonstrate an innovative approach, creativity, collaboration and risk taking.

Underpinning all these attributes, the key foundation must be a positive attitude: a 'can-do' approach, a readiness to take part and contribute, openness to new ideas and a drive to make these happen.

Source: Adapted from CBI, 2009: 8, used with permission

Not surprisingly, these core skills are echoed by other employers we spoke to.

Allie Whelan, Director of LeapUK, an organisation specialising in recruitment and placement of graduates, looked beyond academic qualifications and stressed the importance of social skills and determination. She told us:

> No matter what you have on paper, your soft skills need to present a confident and capable self for you to become employable. You need to be confident in yourself, be an incredibly good listener, and have good speaking skills. You need to have self-assurance, to be passionate and to show that you want to find out more – to learn and grow. You need to show that you are able to do become the stars of the future. (Authors' interview)

Important as technical ability and academic qualifications may be, we are also reminded by Patrick Goh, Head of Global HR People and Organisation Development, Tearfund, that

> With 'employability', the clue is in the name – how to be sufficiently attractive to an organisation that they want to work with you. It is symbiotic. It is not just what the organisation is looking for, but also how the individual presents themselves – how they align with the needs of the organisation, especially their aptitude and realistic aspirations. This means that it may not be the most technically brilliant person who gets the job, but the one who shares our values and demonstrates their aptitudes and aspirations. (Authors' interview)

The key messages are that we need to start early with developing employability – in discussions with everyone we spoke to in preparing for the book, we were reminded that exploring ideas, even from the first year at university, would not be too early. Indeed, some of our respondents suggested that school had an important role to get students thinking about the future and, importantly, getting initial experience of the workplace.

Starting early may enable the lucky ones – perhaps a minority of lucky ones – to find that they have developed contacts (networks) and an interest in fields of work that will last them a lifetime. For others, starting early will mean going down the wrong path. Either way it means gaining work experience, exploring options and, if necessary, readjusting to what you really want to do. It is about finding out where you want to go.

In addition to the academic review of employability it is helpful to consider how employers have responded in research undertaken for this book. In the Exhibit 1.2 we summarise some employer views on how organisations consider employability, defined in organisational language. Their comments were echoed by employers in the private sector and social enterprises.

Exhibit 1.2

Employability (1): Confidence, Lifelong Learning and Soft Skills

Employability is about getting into graduate-level roles and feeling confident in furthering one's future career. Employability prepares people for graduate-level work and lifelong learning. Within the academic curriculum it is very much about working effectively in teams, effective presentations, time management, delivering results, interpersonal skills and developing confidence. All of these are critical in developing employability skills. **Professor Julie McLeod, Pro Vice-Chancellor (Student Experience), Oxford Brookes University**

Soft Skills, Self-assurance and Passion

No matter what you have on paper, your soft skills need to present a confident and capable self for you to become employable. You need to be an incredibly good listener and have good speaking skills. You need to have the self-assurance to be passionate and show that you want to find out more – to learn and grow. You need to show that you are able to become a star of the future. **Allie Whelan, Director LeapUK**

Standing Out, Soft Skills, Going Above and Beyond

Employability is really demonstrating whatever skills or experiences you have that make you stand out – crucially, those that are relevant and sought after by the potential employer. It is also about hunger and passion for the company and role you are applying for. In order to be able to do both of those things, a candidate needs to have a level of intellectual curiosity that goes above and beyond in many walks of life, academic and otherwise. Communication skills will be key in terms of articulating all of this effectively in an interview and also proving that you will be effective with clients, team members and so on. **Sarah Harper, Goldman Sachs Investment Bank**

Getting the Right Experience on Your CV

Your CV must show how you have the skills and experience to perform a role. Perhaps the hardest thing is getting the experience and being able to demonstrate that you can do the job. Employability is also about building on skills and experience for longer-term development. **Ben Palmer, Christian Aid**

Source: Authors' interviews

In conclusion, employers see employability as:

- technical and academic skills are 'givens' (so you need to ensure that yours are as good);
- strong interpersonal skills;
- values which can be seen to be aligned with those of the organisation to which you are applying.

Barriers to Employability

Whether you plan to work in the UK or elsewhere, it is as well to be aware of the barriers to employability. We are not simply referring to competition for roles or availability of job opportunities. Instead, it is important to be aware of barriers which may be based on organisational discrimination or employer assessments about graduate job readiness.

Studies (e.g. Rivera, 2015; International Labour Organisation (ILO) 2011; and publications from the Employment and Human Rights Commission) all report that socio-economic class and background contribute to employment practices. In the USA, Lauren Rivera's (2015) study highlights the practicalities of how elite organisations (especially investment banks and top law firms) concentrate their recruitment efforts on a small number of top US universities. Rivera shows that for those who attend universities outside the golden few, it is difficult to get your CV onto a 'consideration' list, let alone be shortlisted for interview.

Does the same happen elsewhere, including in the UK? Our experience is that many employers would deny this, or at the very least be non-committal. However, as with Rivera's findings in the USA, there is anecdotal evidence that UK employers see UK universities in a pecking order. If you doubt this, then consider where employers invest most funding in sponsorship, entertainment, recruitment fairs and networking visits, and their underlying preferences for particular universities become more apparent. Indeed, this informal evidence from our own discussions with employers was strongly supported by the findings of the Social Mobility and Child Poverty Commission (2015) (sometimes referred to as the Milburn Commission, as Alan Milburn chaired the Commission Board). The Commission found that the UK Russell Group Universities were more actively targeted by the elite UK firms, and that candidates were more likely to be successful from Russell Group Universities. Despite these findings our discussions with a range of employers, anecdotal as they may be, suggested that their definitions of elite universities were actually restricted to only four or five UK universities.

But whether or not these pecking orders exist, your focus on employability should not be undermined. Even if you do not enter an 'elite' organisation, there are many demanding and rewarding opportunities for which you can compete – and compete on a level playing field.

Furthermore, although a wide range of discriminatory practices (whether based on gender, age, disability, religion, sexuality, ethnicity or even HIV/AIDS) are now unlawful in making selection decisions in the UK and many countries internationally, there is still evidence that discrimination continues. For example, within the UK, Ministry of Justice figures for 2012–2013 suggest that at least 19 per cent of cases referred to Employment Tribunals are alleged breaches of UK equality laws (Ministry of Justice, 2012). Furthermore, *Business in the Community' Race into Work* report (2015) found that employment outcomes for Black Asian and Minority Ethnic (BAME) UK graduates were still disproportionately poorer than for UK white graduates, and that this was possibly based on unconscious bias on behalf of recruiters. In Chapters 6 and 7 we will discuss these issues in more detail. In the meantime, we would emphasise that these are issues to be aware of – but not to accept as limitations for your own employment outlooks. .

So, bombarded with this information, is having a degree even worth it? If you have finished a degree course this may not be a question you want to hear, even if you found the experience intrinsically worthwhile and especially if you are currently finding career employment difficult to achieve. Gary Burtless, writing for the Brookings Institute (2013), investigated American education achievement levels and capability to remain in the workforce. He found that in the 1990s, of those men aged 62–74 who dropped out of high school education, only 20 per cent were currently still employed whereas 60 per cent of those with doctorates or professional degrees were still employed. Though less marked for women and those with first degrees, there were similar benefits in being able to remain in the workforce longer. It is believed that the effects of higher education are similar for Europe. Of course, there is a difference between being able to be in the workforce longer, driven by work satisfaction, and having to be in the workforce longer, driven by economic need. Equally, we do not know whether the social and economic contexts which were the background to these results will be the same in the future. Nevertheless, at a time when we will all need to work longer before retirement, Burtless (2013) comments, 'People with college and advanced degrees tend to remain in the workforce longer.'

For many graduates the message is clear: as well as performing well in their degree subjects, a range of additional attributes need to be achieved in order to be truly competitive in the graduate job market.

Exhibit 1.3

Employability (2)

A perspective from within the NHS with Jane Hadfield, Head of Learning & Development, Human Resource & Development Directorate, North Bristol NHS Trust

Work readiness is critically important – technical skills and behaviours, values and ethics which align with those of the Trust. North Bristol Trust places a high priority on recruiting people with the right values and ethics for working together and having patient needs at the heart of everything we do. This is not only important for our Trust, but to meet the requirements of the NHS Constitution too, with its emphasis on employee and employer values.

Technical skills are equally important as values: the NHS places a heavy reliance on skills and knowledge. Within North Bristol Trust, two-thirds of our 10,000 employees are graduates, and many of these also have higher degrees.

But we need to be cautious to ensure that even the brightest academic candidates are well balanced for the world of work in social skills and values; if they are not, it will limit their opportunities. One of the challenges for young people is their tendency to have self-limiting beliefs – improving their self-confidence is important.

So in recruiting new graduates we look for work readiness – technical ability, of course, but with the right values for good organisational fit.

For nursing graduates we had found historically that they were not fully prepared for the workplace. To address this, a transitional development programme was established to enhance workplace skills.

Source: Authors' research

Employability Model

We have seen a number of different perspectives of employability, whether from theorists or current educational or employer practitioners.

Each has an important and valid perspective, but we want to propose a model which is relevant at graduation but also beyond, taking us well into our professional lives. Therefore the six elements we see as essential for sustained employability are: managed applications; qualifications; continued learning; experience; self-belief; interpersonal skills (Figure 1.2).

This section introduces each element in further detail and shows where we discuss the issues in more depth later in the book.

FIGURE 1.2   Employability model

Manage Your Applications

The most serious criticisms which employers make about work applications are that they are generic: that the same application could be used to do anything, anywhere, and do not address the needs of that organisation; that they do not answer the questions or follow the process on the application form; and that they have grammatical and spelling errors in them.

Applying for a role is a very time-consuming process. But additional tailoring and focus for your application should mean that you have fewer applications to submit in the longer term.

Apply for roles early. Make the most of vacation internships (some employers, especially in the financial and professional services sectors, will offer graduate roles well ahead of actual graduation on the basis of successful internships). Too many graduates still apply for roles later in the graduate recruitment cycle. You should have your application details ready in the summer before your final year of study, and must be ready to apply (as well as study) in your first semester of your final year.

We cover this topic in more detail in Chapter 3.

Qualifications

You will have spent a significant proportion of your life to date chasing achievement through qualifications and grades. Nobody can take away from you this very significant achievement. The challenge is competing for work with the number of people who will have done as well as you, better than you, and worse than you in grade terms.

Qualifications are a prerequisite for consideration for employment, but they are only one of six factors that will take you to interview and appointment. For *a limited number of employers* the wrong class of degree, or even the wrong university, may prevent you from being shortlisted. For *most employers* even high university qualifications will not get you shortlisted unless you have a robust application, reflecting the six elements of employability that we discuss here.

Continued Learning

Continued learning – and being able to demonstrate and articulate that learning – may be less critical to demonstrate at graduation, but is essential for later development. Learning may be through developing competences, additional study (especially professional qualifications and registration) or continuing professional development (CPD). Don't forget to include learning from gap-year experiences, temporary employment and volunteering.

We cover these topics in more detail in Chapter 5.

Experience

How do we get experience when it is the initial experience we are seeking in the first place?

The two ways to address this are:

- Seek to get relevant experience as early as possible. Your final years at school and your first year at university are not too early. This may be through work applications or voluntary activities.
- Show that wider experience you have obtained from other work, voluntary activity, work in clubs and societies and sports achievements, leadership and coaching have contributed to your relevant experience, and that this is transferable to your application with that employer.

Self-belief

Sustained self-belief is critical in finding the right career route, and role, for your future. For many it may also be the most challenging part of employability, especially in challenging job markets. Henry Ford is quoted as saying 'Whether you think you can, or you think you can't – you're right.' But he is also reported to have said that 'Vision without execution is just hallucination.' So, even with a clear idea of what we want to do in life, determined application with self-belief is important.

In defining self-belief we include:

- **Passion** for your chosen area: *every employer we have spoken to* has said that this is the distinguishing feature of a successful candidate. Passion reflects your internal belief for a particular role and your ability to demonstrate and articulate this clearly.

  Your 'passion' must also demonstrate that your values are aligned – and can be seen to be aligned – with your potential employer. In his report on the Mid Staffordshire NHS Trust, where an estimated 400 to 1,200 hospital patients died because of poor care between 2005 and 2009, Sir Robert Francis recommended the future need for NHS values and that these should be part of future NHS employment contracts. Wherever we apply, our values need to be aligned with those of the employer – work life is miserable, and often short, where values are misaligned.

- **Overcoming barriers**: to what extent your self-belief enables you to overcome obvious and less obvious external barriers. This may include the need to recognise – and address – direct or indirect discrimination.

- **Resilience**: the ability to bounce back and continue the search, despite rejection. We have discussed resilience with orchestral musicians, actors and artists. For each, competition amongst similarly gifted performers means frequent (and at times abrupt) failure at auditions. We have met teachers who have finished their training but could not immediately find teaching posts, pilots who successfully completed their initial flying training but were then made redundant from the Royal Air Force (RAF), and a psychologist who worked for several years as a care assistant – despite these setbacks, all went on to successful careers. If we can retain the resilience and passion of these graduates, and learn from failure or rejection, we will have stronger and more focused future applications.

- **Adjustment** recognising that if you are to achieve your plans there may be more than one way to do this. Plans may need to be adjusted for timing, where you plan to work, who you plan to work with and so on.

We cover these topics in more detail in Chapters 6 and 7.

Interpersonal Skills

As basic as it may seem, employers require good interpersonal skills – to relate well to other individuals and to relate well across the organisation. Reinforcing this point, Jane Hadfield, Head of Learning & Development, North Bristol NHS Trust, considered values and personal skills as equally important as academic and technical skills in the recruitment process.

We include further discussion about interpersonal skills in Chapter 3.

Conclusion

In this chapter we have had a brief overview of the world of work and what it is to be considered 'employable'.

Making yourself employable starts early – certainly from year one of university, but ideally before that too. All work experience can be used to construct your employability profile.

Recognise that employers will look for passion in your desire to work for them.

For some, there will be early setbacks – resilience will be required.

ACTION

Having read this chapter, we suggest that you think about the following action points:

- If you haven't done so already, be determined to develop your employability. It is never too early to start.
- Using the model for employability in this chapter, be objective, and check off how your employability strategy has strengths or gaps. How will you close those gaps?
- Check *now* the employability support available through your university, college or school – many of these are excellent in providing support and some offer accredited programmes to help your employability.
- Make and maintain contact with your careers service. They will not 'tell you what type of job you should do'; rather, as you develop your plans, they will guide you to information about your chosen job opportunities and help you develop realistic plans and skills to achieve those.

Further Reading

If you are studying graduate employability or simply looking at the types of selection procedures which you will face, then Social Mobility and Child Poverty Commission's 'A qualitative evaluation of non-educational barriers to the elite professions' (2015) gives a further research-based perspective of the UK job market and assessment methods used for graduate recruitment. It is a useful addition to the contents of this study guide. The report is available at www.gov.uk/government/uploads/system/uploads/attachment_data/file/434791/A_qualitative_evaluation_of_non-educational_barriers_to_the_elite_professions.pdf.

Similarly, if you are studying employability there is a wide range of journal literature to which you can refer, including self-rating scales for employability. In this chapter we have summarised only the key readings.

To find out more about graduate employment prospects, including the more nuanced arguments about how UK graduates fare, see CIPD (2015b) Over-qualification and skills mismatch in the graduate labour market.

Look out for relevant websites from the professional bodies covering your intended future career paths. These will help you understand contemporary issues affecting that profession, and some may also have details about internships and job opportunities.

Keep an eye on the graduate job market, either by what you read in the press or look at press releases from the Association of Graduate Careers Advisory Services (AGCAS) at www.agcas.org.uk/.

Keep in touch with opportunities at your university. If you are studying away from home, visit the university near your home. How different, or similar, is the support available for those students? You will not normally be able to use their facilities for advice and guidance, but looking at the information they have may give you fresh insights which you can follow up later.

2

Changing Patterns of Career

In this chapter we consider what is meant by the term 'career', the stages we go through during our career journey and the influences on our career, including psycho-social factors, age and the changes in society within which our careers are formed and reformed.

In many ways we are defined by our work. In social situations when we meet people for the first time we may be asked, 'And what do you do?'. We are often judged by the worthiness of our response to the question. So to be a Lifeboatman may be good, but to be a traffic warden not so good, Yet they are both important in maintaining order and safety in our society. Sociologists and marketers seek to classify us, our expected behaviours and our spending patterns according to what we do or don't do. Even motorcar insurance companies classify our accident risk according to our occupation.

Little wonder that we invest so much time and effort into work. And with that investment we would do well to find work in which we are happy, competent and feel that we are being appropriately rewarded and fairly treated.

For many starting out on their career journeys, the type of role they are currently undertaking is unlikely to be similar to the role they will find themselves in at the end of their careers. At the very least, the pace of the technological change will mean that the ways in which we work now will be very different later in our careers. What is difficult to predict (and so justifies the continued commitment we have to lifelong learning) is what shape future changes will take. Even prominent thinkers in the past have been spectacularly wrong in predicting the future.

Take the example of the eminent economist, John Maynard Keynes, who wrote in 1930 that we were suffering from 'growing-pains': the pain of very rapid technological change and adjustments between economic periods. Little seems to have changed since then, either in the pace of change or in adjusting between economic periods, both nationally and globally. But Keynes believed that by now we could be working as little as 15 hours per week. He assumed that technological change would have introduced so much productivity into the economy that we would simply need to share out the work that remained.

Keynes' predictions have not come true – at least not yet. Instead, if we work for 40 years and 38 hours a week (as many of us still do), we will spend 77,000 hours at work. Furthermore, the issue of extended working hours is regarded as such a contemporary social problem that European legislation restricts the working week to a maximum of 48 hours per week, usually averaged over a 17-week period (European Parliament, 2003).

But as well as how long we work, it is clear that what we do and the way we do it will also change. As we see the potential and prospect of driverless cars, and delivery by drones, equally fundamental forces will change the pattern of future work. These factors may include:

- **Global growth**: We have already seen the growth of the Peoples' Republic of China and of India. Their combined populations of 2.6 billion dwarf those of the USA (319 million) and the European Union (507 million). On their current trajectories, China and India will continue in importance both as centres of manufacturing and learning – indeed, they are expected to produce 40 per cent of the world's graduates by 2020 (OECD, 2012). As they grow we can expect growth in the supply, demand and competition for goods and services.

  But it is not only China and India that are growing. Other economies are also increasing, both in manufacturing capacity and demand for goods and services as well as in education. The OECD expects there to be 204 million adults aged 25–34 by 2020, compared with 91 million in the year 2000 (OECD, 2012).

- **Technological change**: Much of the technological change we take for granted now was not even available 10 years ago. In 2005 only birds 'tweeted'. Since its inauguration in 2006, Twitter usage is now measured in the hundreds of millions of tweeted messages daily. But in addition to its usage by individuals, the growth of Twitter has delivered two major impacts. The first is the influence it has had on social media and news feeds – traditional news media uses Twitter both as a source of emerging stories and as integration into its own media releases. At the same time social media represents a major threat to traditional broadcast and print media, especially for younger generations of users. The second major impact that Twitter has had is in developing an organisation with a significant stock market valuation: on 1 July 2015, Twitter's market valuation was US$ 23 billion – and that for an organisation – and a concept – which had not existed 10 years previously. (Social media is also important with job-hunting skills, and in Chapter 3 we share best practice on using LinkedIn for job searches.)

  The rise of Twitter – and other brands which have experienced similar market growth – is only one obvious sign of how technological changes impact on our daily lives. Global connectivity to the World Wide Web, now estimated as 3 billion, is expected to continue to rise, bringing new knowledge and new economic opportunities. Technological 'jumps' also mean that some economies which could not benefit from technology improvements now can do so. For example, in Africa, despite a previous lack of infrastructure, mobile phone technology is increasingly used for a range of applications, including healthcare (Kimenyi, 2015). Emerging technology being developed in the UK may one day mean that the same phones can be recharged using urine (UWE, 2012), so adding more value to 'spending a penny'.

- **Demographic changes**: By 2015 the United Nations (UN) noted that global population had reached 7.3 billion, an increase of 1 billion over 12 years (UN, 2015: 1). It is expected to reach 8.5 billion in 2030, 9.7 billion in 2050 and 11.2 billion by 2100 (UN, 2015: 2). It is also forecast that life expectancy will increase from 70 years in 2010–2015 to 77 years in 2045–2050 and to 83 years in 2095–2100, with the most significant increases in life expectancy coming from Africa (UN, 2015: 6). Against these expectations of increasing populations globally, Europe's population is actually expected to decline – and grow older – following a trend already seen in other countries, such as Japan. Little wonder, therefore, that in many developed countries concern is expressed about the cost of care of the elderly and that retirement ages have increased, leading to longer working lives – your working lives – before retirement.

These global, technological and demographic changes, combined with other social and political changes globally, will present an uncertain future for the context of careers. Already some commentators are forecasting an 'hour-glass' effect (e.g. see Sissons, 2011). The hour-glass effect anticipates that economies will become increasingly based on knowledge. As a result, there will be good jobs and bad jobs. High-skill, high-paid professional and managerial jobs will be created, as will low-wage service roles, but middle-wage occupations would be squeezed out (so the distribution of jobs and wages would resemble an hour-glass).

The last few decades have also seen a rise in outsourced jobs; for example, call centres based off-shore and airline catering outsourced (some airlines even outsource flight crews). A visitor to some hightech 'just-in-time' manufacturing units will also see manufacturing parts being delivered to assembly positions by external logistics specialists. The manufacturer's own staff do the assembly and the logistics companies concentrate on delivery of parts or pay hefty penalty charges if they are not delivered. Atkinson (1985) saw the firm as more flexibly structured: as an onion with core, permanent workers at the centre and less permanent and agency workers at the periphery. For permanent core workers, life and salaries may be stable, but for those on the periphery, prospects are nowhere near as certain. Atkinson's model has been debated and critiqued, leaving open the question of how this may apply in the twenty-first century. However, the collapse in 2014 of the UK courier City Link demonstrated how many drivers seen in the streets in City Link vans were actually self-employed. In white-collar roles, interim and contractor work are increasingly seen as career routes in their own right.

Similarly in Japan, the number of workers in non-permanent (non-regular) work has already reached 19.9 million (*Wall Street Journal*, 2015). Elsewhere, websites such as TaskRabbit for manual jobs and Uber for taxi-type services have already led the way in web-based work and services for what is increasingly referred to as the 'gig' economy, where work and services are bought and sold online. There is evidence that the same approach is also being used for white-collar work, especially in services such as IT, health, art and literacy (Cadman, 2015). Boudreau et al. (2015) also see a world where work goes 'beyond employment' and discovered that organisations were finding different ways of getting work achieved without necessarily employing their own people. Bourdeau et al. therefore suggest that organisations should consider getting jobs done by 'workers' – though they may not necessarily be employees of that organisation. The nature of this type of work may be satisfactory for people looking for short-term assignments, but there remain unanswered questions about the long-term growth of this sector and the employment rights and benefits of those who work within it.

Clearly, the competition for entry into large, blue-chip organisations is tough (see, e.g., Connor and Shaw, 2008). Many graduates, whether out of choice or necessity, may therefore prefer to join smaller organisations where graduate development is less structured and less likely to include the levels of job and experience rotation, mentoring and similar development experiences of large organisations. However, there may be significant other benefits in joining the right, smaller organisation, and personal learning and development may be as well managed by the individual as by being driven by the bureaucracy of a larger organisation.

Hogarth et al. (2007) found that whilst the training provided by smaller organisations may be less structured, they often provided earlier opportunities for higher levels of personal responsibility. An example of a smaller organisation which provides nationally recognised excellence in learning and development is South-West London housing provider Richmond Housing Partnership (RHP Group). With approximately 250 employees, RHP has put effort into developing an organisation where everyone is viewed as part of their talent pool and their approach to developing leaders at all levels has led to some significant successes. RHP emphasises the importance of learning in all aspects of their people management and invest over £700 per employee per year on learning and development activities. They offer a blend of technical and behavioural training including role-specific training where it is required, much of it accredited, to give their people CV-enhancing benefit, as well as 'great place to think' events, with external speakers doing short sessions on issues that not only affect the community and housing management provision but are also designed to create better business leaders through sessions about strategy, execution and innovation. As part of their voluntary work, RHP employees are also encouraged to 'give back' to the community, for example as RHP's Digital Champions, training local people in IT skills. RHP's success in this area has been recognised with a number of awards, including Investors in People Gold Standard and the Chartered Institute of Personnel and Development's '2015 Company of the Year Award'. But RHP's emphasis is not provided only for altruistic reasons. Executive Director of Corporate Services, Amina Graham, comments that

> Investing in people development is a business imperative, not a choice; if organisations want to optimise business performance in a sustainable way they need a well-skilled, flexible, curious and highly engaged workforce. (Authors' research)

The benefits of investment in learning is also reflected in their sector-leading customer satisfaction, having a top-20 place in the UK Customer Satisfaction Index in the retail non-food category (coming number one for 'friendliness' in the summer 2015 list, and beating bigger, household names) and for achieving the highest ranking in the sector for creating an innovative, friendly culture.

Not all smaller organisations have the structured and successful commitment to learning and development demonstrated by RHP. However, the RHP experience demonstrates that graduates do not have to look to the larger organisations for excellence in development. Smaller organisations can deliver this just as well – and even better, in the case of RHP.

Exhibit 2.1

Graduate concerns in finding the right career

If you are finding it difficult to think about the right way forward for your future career, you are not alone. Here are some of the concerns expressed by our Employability Panel – and remember, they are already in work.

- Finding career advice and guidance.
- Finding it difficult to identify the right career for me.
- Difficulty proving myself/seeking opportunities to develop my role.
- Gender bias.
- Lack of knowing which career direction to go in.
- Lack of career path.
- If this right for me?

Source: Employability Panel n=50

In summary, work and career remain a very significant part of our lives. Not just those hours actually at work, but the years in preparing ourselves for work through education and interacting with people in work or out of work. Furthermore, the world in which we work is clearly undergoing significant change, for global, technological and demographic reasons. With these factors so prominent in our lives, it is important that we now look in more detail at the topic of career, and in doing so to focus on what we do now and in the future to manage our careers.

The Meaning of 'Career'

'Career' is one of those words which we use so regularly that we perhaps take its actual meaning for granted. An early definition was offered by Hughes:

A series of statutes and clearly defined offices ... subjectively, a
career is the moving perspective in which the person sees his [*sic*]
life as a whole and interprets the meaning of his various attributes,
actions, and the things that happen to him [*sic*]. (1937: 143)

In Hughes' definition, notice that careers in the 1930s were seen as a
male world. For a more up to date definition, Arnold defines career as:

The sequence of employment-related positions, roles, activities, and
experiences encountered by a person. (1997: 16)

In John Arnold's definition, careers are related to employment, but
also go beyond paid employment. Both definitions imply a sense that
'career' is wider than well-paid jobs: they are about meaning (and by
implication, how we live our values), and look at our whole lives –
whether or not that currently includes paid work. Both definitions
also recognise that careers are dynamic and changing.

As we will see in this chapter, the interpretation of what constitutes
a career – especially a successful career – have changed considerably
over the last 20 years, as have the social and economic contexts in
which carers are developed.

However, before we explore those different interpretations of
career, it is useful to recognise that 'career' goes through a number of
development stages, as summarised in Table 2.1.

Career at Different Life Stages

Much of the focus on employability has been on being ready for work
at the conclusion of higher education. But, as this book will show,
employability is as much about being ready for the next career move,
at whatever stage of life we are.

What issues may we expect to confront us as we progress through
our careers? Not surprisingly, this has been considered by researchers.
Prominent in explaining issues in career at different stages and times
of life are Donald Super and Daniel Levinson, whose findings on career
stages from adolescence onwards are summarised in Table 2.2.

The work on career stages linked with age bands by Super, Levinson
and others has been critically reviewed, particularly in relation to the
assumptions it makes about age bands. Furthermore, the models tend
to be male dominated and do not help to explain women's careers
when, for example, returning to work after childbirth. By setting
expectations at various ages, there is a risk of reinforcing age-related
stereotypes; in later years, Super put a greater emphasis on where a

TABLE 2.1   Summary of stages and development of career

Stage	Characteristics
Explore	Thinking about future roles, finding and losing opportunities.
Establish	Settling into a role which is, or is near, to what you want to do.
Develop and grow	A steady period of career growth, typically including widening experience and competence development, often linked with promotion.
	Development may be a smooth line or fragmented.
Career break	Can come at any time in career. Typically can be for parental or caring responsibilities, travel or sabbatical leave. Key challenges are to remain up to date and well networked.
	It is better to go into a career break with a realistic plan of how the career break will be concluded, rather than an open-ended break. In the post-financial service's economic depression some employers used enforced sabbaticals and career breaks as a mechanism to lay off workers without losing their skills once the economy started to recover.
Burnout	A state of mental weariness (Freudenberger, 1974; Schaufeli et al., 2008). Dychtwald et al.(2006) found that sources of frustration included career bottleneck (too few roles in delayered organisations), work–life tensions (parents and/or children), lengthening horizons (in which planned retirement dates became deferred), skills obsolescence and disillusion.
	Burke (1993) noted that feelings from career burnout included emotional exhaustion, depersonalisation (excessive detachment from people and clients in the workplace) and reduced personal accomplishment (in which the employee evaluates personal work performance negatively, feels incompetent and unable to achieve goals). Similarly negative descriptions of burnout were identified by Maslach (1993), who viewed burnout as exhaustion (drained mental resources), cynicism (indifference or a distant attitude towards one's job) and lack of professional efficacy (the tendency to evaluate personal work performance in a negative way, with feelings of insufficiency and poor job-related self-esteem).
Derailment	Derailment occurs when a previously successful career suddenly becomes problematic and unsuccessful. Typical reasons may be personality clash with senior colleagues, health or skills and knowledge no longer as relevant. Derailment can be avoided by good work–life balance, keeping learning up to date and a focus on emotional intelligence.
Plateau	The point in a career where the likelihood of additional hierarchical promotion is very low (Ference et al, 1977: 602). It may be followed by gradual decline in responsibilities. Measures to avoid plateaux are similar as for derailment.
Ending	With career endings (retirement) come new beginnings. UK statistics published in 2013 by the Office for National Statistics showed a marked decline in employment rates for those aged over 50 despite state retirement ages of 60 and 65 for women and men respectively (ONS, 2013: 14). However, longer working lives mean that people entering the UK workforce now can expect to retire at age 68 by 2046, with similar later retirement ages internationally. Again, this puts a renewed emphasis on work–life balance and keeping learning up to date. Later careers may include more part-time working and portfolio careers.

TABLE 2.2   To show career development and age

Super (1957)	Levinson et al. (1978)	Characteristics of different career life stages
Exploration (age 15–24 years)	**Early adulthood (age 20–40)** **Early adult transitions (age 17–20)** Start to think about place in the world, separate from parents, school etc.	Self-concept crystallises through experiment and reality testing. Individuals match interests and capabilities to occupations and apply self-concept roles. Stereotypes refined
Establishment (age 25–44 years) Find a permanent career, opportunities and promotion	**Entering the adult world (age 23–28)** Develop sense of personal identity in work and non-work **Thirties transition (age 29–33)** Evaluate accomplishments of age 20s, and adjust to adopted life structure **Settling down (age 34–39)** Work towards achievement of work goals; commitment to family, work, community	
Maintenance (age 44–64 years) Holding on and maintenance of self-concept and job status. Career choices about staying with current occupation or organisation	**Middle adulthood (age 40–60)** **Mid-life transition (age 40–45)** Evaluate accomplishments of age 30s, and adjust to adopted life structure. Recognise and adjust to limits of achievement and mortality **Entering middle adulthood (age 46–50)** Develop greater stability as questions from earlier stage become part of mindset **Fifties transition (age 51–55)** Raise questions about lifestyle previously adopted **Culmination of middle adulthood (age 56–60)** Answer previous questions and adjust lifestyle choices	Society age norms may start to question age for a particular role (e.g. Lawrence, 1988). Job shift if discomfort with supervision by younger managers (Brewington and Nassar-McMillan, 2000) Loss of colleagues of similar age bands may lead to feelings of work isolation and job dissatisfaction (Gibson and Barron, 2003). Career plateau (Tan and Salomone, 1994)
Decline/ disengagement (age 64+) Mental and physical power decline and pace of work eases back		Individuals seek to develop a self-image and self-concept independent of the workplace (Giannantonio and Hurley-Hanson, 2006) Employment during ages 60s/70s may leave some longer in the maintenance stages (Brewington and Nassar-McMillan, 2000)

person was in the lifecourse, rather than stick to age-based expectations. We should also note that much of the research was undertaken when retirement ages were lower. Despite these criticisms of the age related carer expectations, the models have been reproduced here as a reminder that our perspectives and needs from our career are likely to change as we grow older, and progress through the lifecourse. This reinforces the need to have a sense of longer-term direction as part of our personal ownership of our own employability.

Contemporary Views of Career

We have seen so far that the late twentieth-century view was that careers tended to be hierarchical progression within a limited number of organisations. In contrast, Hassard et al. (2012: 571) note the wide body of research covering the last 20 years, which show that one reason that careers have changed is the widespread introduction of flatter and less hierarchical organisation forms. These are often the result of organisations bringing greater focus on their core business and process re-engineering. As a consequence there are fewer managerial roles (delayering), and the process has been linked with reduced work commitment, high levels of job mobility, reduced job security and reduced organisation loyalty (Hassard et al., 2012: 573; Heckscher, 1995).

Against this background it is argued that future career patterns will be much harder to discern, although they are likely to have the following features:

Later start of 'career' and longer working lives: The first decade of the twenty-first century has seen higher proportions of young people entering higher education, with some evidence of fragmented career starts. At the same time, working lives are likely to be longer as retirement dates increase to age late-60s.

Boundaryless careers: Boundaryless careers are also described as 'portfolio' (see below), or 'protean post-corporate'. By some they are seen to be less secure than a less conventionally organisation-based career. For others they become more liberating and as commitment ties may be loosened, less dominated by one particular organisation. Boundaryless careers (Arthur and Rousseau, 1996) are those which (for whatever reason) go across different organisations. Protean careers (Hall, 1976, 2002; Hall and Associates, 1996) are those where the individual has consciously decided to self-manage their future careers without dependence on a single organisation. Briscoe et al. (2006) pointed out that these types of career, which were regarded as radical or unusual, were becoming more widespread.

Portfolio careers: Portfolio careers (usually attributed to Handy, 1991, and sometimes used inter-changeably with boundaryless careers) are a situation where an individual has more than one 'job' packaged together to provide the equivalent of a full-time working role. These may be part-time roles, freelance, fixed-term contracts and sometimes also include significant voluntary activity. Even well-established professional careers have been linked with the possibility of working on a portfolio basis in the future; for example, articles in the *British Medical Journal* (BMJ) have discussed the attractions of portfolio careers for hospital consultants[1] and general medical practitioners.[2]

PRACTICAL APPLICATION

Not everyone is suited to a boundaryless or portfolio career, and finance can be precarious during this time of your working life. You will need to be a great networker, resilient to manage uncertainty, clear about what competences and skills you can offer, and be able to work independently or with others with equal ease.

Portfolio careers carry the risk of spreading yourself too thin to make substantive progress in one direction. However, they are an excellent way to gain experience, try out different roles and organisations, and for networking. Portfolio careers may be particularly useful for those in early career (testing new situations pending a conventional role) or in late career pending career ending.

Exhibit 2.2

Examples of Portfolio Careers from our Employability Panel

From our Employability Panel, here are a few examples of early portfolio careers:

Art and Antiquities Dealer: now self-employed entrepreneur (see case study in Chapter 3).

Classical Musician: with roles in several different orchestra and music groups; includes short-term work.

Marketer: voluntary work (e.g. music festival, charity shop); short-term marketing roles in variety of media prior to Digital Media Executive appointment as career role.

Conservation work: undertaken as voluntary work; working as a street cleaner in the meantime to fund conservation work.

---

[1]Pathiraja and Wilson, 2011.
[2]Crawley, 1996, 313: S2–7065.

Marine engineer:– now fully qualified, but after leaving an automotive degree course, apprenticeship in musical instrument making and sales.

Teaching: many examples of teachers who started working in after-school clubs, teaching assistants and supply teachers prior to appointment as full-time teachers. In the UK, Teach First[3] also offers an opportunity to graduates who are looking for early teaching and commercial experience. Internationally, several countries have similar schemes.

Critics of these views of the contemporary and future career suggest that the risks of career fragmentation may be exaggerated, recognising that whilst there may be grounds for work- and career-related anxiety, these may be counterbalanced by work with greater freedom and less constrained by a single organisation. Indeed, the existence and lack of clarity of the new career has itself been criticised (Inkson et al., 2012). In particular, it is suggested that there is not yet sufficient empirical evidence that the new career is widespread and that there remain differences in career types across different sectors (Tempest et al., 2004).

The Possibility of Better Gender Balance

Despite the existence of equal pay and equality legislation in the UK (for over 40 years) and many other countries, there continues to be inequality for women in the workplace. Women often receive lower pay in the labour market (the International Labour Office 2011 reports that women's pay is still 70–90 per cent the level of men's pay, globally); there is under-representation of women in senior roles (the UK Government's Department for Business Innovation and Skills reported in 2015 an improvement of 25 per cent women's representation on FTSE boards, but that there is still progress to be made) and fractured women's careers linked with childbirth and childcare (although the *Guardian* reported in 2015 that Sweden now requires fathers to take – not swap with the mother – one-third of parental leave on the birth of a child).

---

[3]For details go to www.teachfirst.org.uk/.

Manage Your Employee Brand: The Increased Responsibility for Self-development of Career

As we have seen already in this book, the old paternal style of an organisation taking care of you and your career is rapidly disappearing. Some talent management programmes aspire to offer career and development support for the chosen few. In its place, the individual will need to take personal responsibility for their career and lifelong employability and workplace learning. The book is intended to help you with this, and we discuss this in more detail in Chapter 5.

Generational Differences in Career

In the previous section we saw that researchers such as Super and Levinson had focused their attentions on career stage in relation to age. More recent attention has considered whether there are generational differences in how individuals view their careers, based not on age but on the society contexts of their formative years and the employment market as they started work. These society contexts are seen to be important because our early, formative years are believed to have a deep impact on how our attitudes, beliefs and values are developed, after which we tend to become more resistant to change (Krosnick and Alwin, 1989; Alwin and Krosnick, 1991). Examples of society contexts and formative events may include World War II and post-war austerity (Veterans); the threat of nuclear war, the Cold War and the assassination of President Kennedy (Baby Boomers); society's renewed focus on wealth, youth and family (Generation X); and the 9/11 destruction of the Twin Towers and the emergence of 'digital natives' (Generation Y).

Different generations and their career drivers and preferences have been categorised as follows:

Veterans (those born between 1925 to 1942):– Orientation to work suggests they are loyal, work hard and prefer the status quo; other research suggests that Veterans build tacit knowledge (experience) relevant to their organisation (Eisner, 2005).

Baby Boomers (those born between 1945 and 1964, and entering the workforce from the mid-1960s):– Their values are said to be freedom from pressures to conform and seeking opportunities to learn new things (Jurkiewicz, 2000). As with Veterans, Baby Boomers are more likely than their successors to have 'bounded careers' (remaining in one occupational type or with the same employer) (Dries et al., 2008). They were more likely than other generations to find career-entry roles relatively easily, and did not have clear career goals (Lyons et al., 2014).

Generation X (those joining the work force in the early 1980s):– Their values are distrustful of authority and more loyal to their occupation/professions than to their employers (Johnson and Lopes, 2008); good communicators and problem solvers (Eisner, 2005). Careers are more likely to be mobile because of instability of employment opportunity (Dries et al., 2008).

Generation Y or Millennials (those born in the 1980s, entering the work force in the late 1990s):– Their work values are said to be ambitious and they are eager to advance with earnings and status (Lyons et al., 2014). They are said to be more entrepreneurial than previous generations (Crumpacker and Crumpacker, 2007), needy, impatient (Johnson and Lopes, 2008), lacking focus and direction and low in problem solving skills (Smola and Sutton, 2002).

Critique of the Generation Approach to Career

The generational descriptors may have an initial appeal in under-standing our career perspectives and attitudes, but the approach has been heavily critiqued. For example, the cut-off dates for each genera-tion require justification rather than anecdote (Parry, 2014). The 'formative events' in each generation category and the chronological periods they cover are probably not applicable globally because soci-ety and international events have different impacts across the world (Yu and Miller, 2005; Parry et al., 2012). An alternative perspective to age or generation is that a person's perspective may be formed by their location in the lifecourse (Bengtson et al., 2005). Furthermore, as Rhodes (1983) would point out, without long-term studies of popu-lations as they became older it is difficult to say whether age or gen-eration affect workers' lives as they grow older.

PRACTICAL APPLICATION

We have considered perspectives of career from the point of view of career stage development, age and generation. If you look at these approaches you will, no doubt, find that some characteristics fit your own perspectives, whilst others do not. This is inevitable – we are all different. Despite the national and global events which may affect us all, our cultures, life experiences and occu-pational preferences differ. Which approach – age, our position in the lifecourse or generation – is most likely to reflect our attitudes to career? The research evidence is mixed. However, by recognising that these differences exist, our understanding of our own employability matures and is better able to make sense of the differences we may encounter in the workplace and how our own attitudes develop as we become older.

Psychometric Tests and Career

All of this begs the question of what your future career plans are and how you will prepare for them – in other words, looking at your own employability as a long-term project, not simply an issue to worry about from graduation.

For many, the types of jobs and experiences which are taken in the early years after graduation are often different from graduate careers in the past (Connor and Shaw, 2008). For some this may initially also mean that they are working in roles which previously did not require graduate qualifications nor offered graduate equivalent rewards (Connor and Shaw, 2008). There is also evidence that organisations have many different approaches both to recruiting graduates and developing them, even within the same organisation. In a case study, albeit within their own company, O'Donnell et al. (2008) stressed the importance of experiential learning and mentoring in addition to more conventional development activities. Furthermore, there is very mixed evidence about the value of joining a graduate development programme within an organisation contrasted with the opportunities arising from direct entry to a role, whether it 'requires' graduate level qualifications or not. For example, whilst Hayman and Lorman (2004) argue that graduate development schemes have become more popular and offer faster career progression, this does not always mean that those graduates are necessarily more committed to the organisation (Cappelli, 2001), nor that they are any more satisfied with their careers (McDermott et al., 2006).

What then are the implications for graduates now seeking to develop their careers? Given the changing patterns of career, what do you expect from your own? Perhaps you are still thinking about what you want to do, or more concerned about finding that first job? Alternatively, you may be at a crossroads in your career and thinking about changing.

For those still thinking about what they want to do, psychometric tests may help. In this section we review some of the more commonly used psychometric tests which may help you clarify what you want from your career. Of these tests, Schein's (1990) questionnaire-based test is amongst the best known. Schein looks at eight career anchors:

1. **Technical/functional**: this suggests that you want to develop your technical skills to the maximum possible levels. Although you may be happy to manage others using similar technical skills, you would not wish to move into more general management areas, preferring instead to remain in the area where you are technically well suited.
2. **General management**: the desire to reach a level in the organisation where you will become responsible for integrating the work of others and become responsible for overall results.

3. **Autonomy/independence**: the ability to organise and do your own work, in the way you want to do it.
4. **Stability/security**: the need to ensure that your work, whatever it is, provides personal and financial stability and security. This may also include employment stability and a sense that you have achieved an appropriate level in society.
5. **Entrepreneurial creativity**: building and running your own organisation and willing to take the pressure, and sometimes failures, in achieving this.
6. **Service/dedication to cause**: work that adds value to other people or causes.
7. **Pure challenge**: addressing and resolving tough problems.
8. **Lifestyle**: balancing family and personal needs with work.

(Adapted and summarised from Schein, 1990)

Since Schein's original work, a ninth factor, Internationalism, has been added to some tests, based on the work of Suutari and Taka (2004). Internationalism suggests that there are some who are excited at the prospect of working within international contexts and that this is sufficiently strong to be a career anchor or trait. Cerdin and Bird (2008) suggest that in addition to looking at internationalism in isolation, some of Schein's original traits can be used in combination to understand whether an individual would be happy working overseas; for example, a high stability/security score under Schein's test may not sit comfortably with an international career. Other researchers, such as Baruch (2004), have proposed career anchors such as employability or spiritual purpose.

An alternative test to help you reflect on career drivers is John Holland's (1977 and 1997) hexagonal model. Holland worked from the 1950s as a careers counsellor and looked at career (vocation) choice as being an expression of personality, based on one of six types of jobs:

1. **Realistic**: prefer action more than thought and concrete problems rather than abstract thinking; also prefer mechanical and physical activity in their work.
2. **Investigative**: strong scientific outlook, seeking out information and data, tend to prefer to work on their own and dislike routine and repetition.
3. **Artistic**: prefer aesthetics and opportunity for self-expression, including music, drama, painting and writing.
4. **Social**: desire to meet and work with other people; socially at ease; caring; teaching.
5. **Enterprising**: enjoy selling and leading; competitive; may dislike spending a long time on detail.
6. **Conventional**: enjoy detail, data management and accuracy.

Holland organised these six types into a hexagon. As we have seen in other career models, where personality can be aligned with role requirements the job holder is more likely to find job satisfaction and wellbeing. Holland (1997) then correlated these personality types with traits, life goals and values. For example, 'Realistic' is linked with traits of being hard-headed, unassuming, practical and dogmatic, with life goals of inventing or becoming an outstanding athlete and values of freedom, ambition, intellectual and self-control. Similarly, 'Social' would be linked with traits of being friendly, sociable, understanding, extrovert and persuasive, with life goals such as helping others, teaching, therapy and values of equality, helpfulness, forgiveness and self-respect.

Holland's career/vocational preference types have been widely used and have formed the basis for extensive additional research, and some researchers have suggested additional types. For those seeking to make sense of their life goals Holland's hexagon may help, even if it does not cover the detail of particular job roles or organisation types. Arnold (2004) noted that Holland's work and supporting self-review questionnaire has been widely used, although tests had shown that the links between test results and individual work satisfaction are not as closely matched as may have been expected.

Myers Briggs and Personality Type

Myers Briggs is a widely known and used personality indicator. It is not intended as a career indicator test, but may still enable you to reflect on your personality and what you may most want for a career. Myers Briggs balances an individual against four type ranges:

1. **Extrovert (E) or Introvert (I)**: Preference for the 'outer world' (extraversion) or 'inner world' (introversion).
2. **Sensing (S) or Intuition (N)**: Preference to focus on the basic information taken in (sensing) or preference to interpret and add meaning (intuition).
3. **Thinking (T) or Feeling (F):** Preference to look first at logic and consistency (thinking) or first look at the people and special circumstances (feeling).
4. **Judging (J) or Perceiving (P)**: Preference to get things decided (judging) or preference to stay open to new information and options (perceiving).

From these four ranges a personality can be profiled into one of 16 different types (see Table 2.3).

TABLE 2.3   Myers-Briggs personality types

ISTJ	ISFJ	INFJ	INTJ
ISTP	ISFP	INFP	INTP
ESTP	ESFP	ENFP	ENTP
ESTJ	ESFJ	ENFJ	ENTJ

Note: E = Extrovert, I = Introvert, S = Sensing, N = Intuition, T = Thinking, F = Feeling

Source: Myers & Briggs Foundation, 2015

A very useful website run by the Myers and Briggs Foundation gives a detailed breakdown on these personality types and is readily accessible.[4]

PRACTICAL APPLICATION

For those who remain genuinely unsure of their future careers, doing psychometric tests such as career anchors may be of value. However, whilst you may have a better understanding of the traits you are looking for within your career, the output of the tests are not designed to identify all the jobs which may fit your profile. Therefore whilst anchors look at traits and preferences, they do not look at the talents, skills and abilities that an individual may offer in a career (Lazarova et al., 2014). Furthermore, there is evidence that as your personal circumstances change, so too may your career anchors change (Chang et al., 2011).

If you think that your needs from work may have changed over time it may be worthwhile doing a career anchors test or other career-related tests. Also very useful, especially if you are in the early stages of your career, is that you will have had a variety of work experiences and be able to give practical insight examples in job applications. This way you will have already been exposed to the practicalities of types of organisation and roles so that you will begin to have understood for yourself what you want from your career. It is also important to recognise that these tests may give you a better idea about your own needs; they don't predict what is required of a particular role, nor do they tell you much about the prospective organisations in which you may work.

Finally, some cautionary advice about doing and using psychometric tests, whether to think about your career preferences, future development or in selection processes. The first is to recognise that they are not foolproof, either at the time you do the tests or for later in your life. Think of them as looking at yourself in the mirror: they give an image, and it is a useful *starting point* to think about your style preferences, where you might develop and how you may come across to others. When you do psychometric tests, avoid thinking that you can second-guess how to get the 'right' results, not least because of the assumptions you are making about what others would regard as the 'right' results. However, it is a good idea to do some of these tests before you start your applications (and periodically throughout

---

[4]For information on MBTI Basics® go to www.myersbriggs.org/my-mbti-personality-type/mbti-basics/.

your career too): this way you will be more confident about what third parties are likely to see in your test results and more informed to discuss your results if required to do so. Recognise that psychometric tests give a view of you at a point in time, they do not 'brand' or label you. You may change or modify your results at a later time, and there are no right or wrong answers.

Thinking About Your Future Career Path

Despite the diversity of ambitions and professions in our Employability Panel and the contemporary career view examined in academic research, future aspirations were often summed up in terms of future progression, feeling valued and being valued in a respected organisation, as shown by this representative employability panel member:

> To have a suitable career, with a steady rate of progression and increasing responsibility. To enjoy my job and feel successful. To be respected within the organisation and have had experience in many different sectors of the business. **Female, Economics Graduate, age 28, Distribution**

What practical advice will help you manage your own career? In Exhibit 2.3, Jenny Body discusses how she developed her own career and rose to be the first woman President of the Royal Aeronautical Society, in what is often regarded as male-dominated profession of aviation and aerospace.

Exhibit 2.3

Managing Your Career Over the Long Term

Here, Jenny Body OBE, FRAeS, aerospace engineer and first woman President of the Royal Aeronautical Society in the UK gives her perspectives and top tips for success. A woman who has risen to the top in what had predominantly been seen as a man's world, Jenny has worked as an aerospace engineer for British Aerospace and then Airbus. Her roles have included specialist roles, such as fly-by-wire, to more general roles as technical manager for wing development and assembly.

Tip one: Be effective in team work. Very often we find ourselves working in multi-disciplinary teams – it is important to understand how to work effectively with others, particularly those whose professional perspectives may be quite different from our own.

Tip two: Develop and maintain your professional pedigree. It's important to have an academic qualification, and when you have that it is equally important to have a relevant professional qualification, and keep up to date with regular continuing professional development (CPD).

Tip three: Want to be promoted? Behave like it now. It is not enough to think to ourselves, 'When I am in the next role, I will behave and act differently': if you want that promotion, behave, without being arrogant, as if you were already in the more senior role.

Tip four: Have a mentor – maybe, have more than one mentor. One may be a professional mentor, the other a personal mentor. Your mentor, ideally, will be outside your line management. A mentor will help you look objectively at your learning needs and future options.

Tip five: Say 'yes' to opportunities – whether roles, secondments or projects. If others see the potential in you, have a reputation for accepting and being successful in new challenges. If you say 'yes', you will be seen as the 'go to' person. If you say 'no', options will start to pass you by.

Tip six: Manage your work–life balance. Work is important and should be fulfilling but has to be balanced with health and relationships in life.

Tip seven: Be vigilant and resilient. Be politically aware and develop resilience – the capability to have setbacks and to respond to those setbacks and come back stronger.

Tip eight: Don't just think about the next job – to have a successful career, be aware of the role after the next job and what you need to do to get it.

Tip nine: Network effectively, and use the value of networking.

Tip ten: Above all, recognise that you are responsible for your career, now and throughout your working life. Your career will not always be about upward moves, as sideways moves into other roles may be important in developing your professional and competences profile

Conclusion

This chapter has discussed the concept of career and shown how very different global economic, technological and social contexts are likely to impact on the pattern of how we understand 'career'.

We have seen that our perspectives of career are likely to change as we grow older. This may reflect changes in age, changes in life-course such as family and so on, or it may reflect your desire to change career entirely later in your working life.

There is no fixed 'pattern' to a successful career start. From preference, or because they have to, some graduates will start their careers on a 'portfolio' basis.

Over what we may expect to be working lives of over 45 years, most of us will need to take personal responsibility for managing our own careers, and with that our long-term employability.

In the next chapter (3), we look at recommended approaches to preparing for work, followed by a chapter (4) on finding work and selection skills.

ACTION

Having read this chapter, we suggest that you think about the following action points:

- How do you see you own career developing?
- What factors will support this? What will obstruct it?
- How will you face these challenges?
- If you drew a graph of your carer over the next 10–20 years, how would it look? What would represent key achievements in your terms? What could cause lower points (in advancement, finance or other reasons), and how will you cope with these?
- Make good use of your university careers service. Check on the website or speak to a careers adviser to understand what the service can offer.
- Resolve now: you are responsible for your career. Organisations may or may not have talent programmes and offer careers advice. Use this book, and other helpful sources, to manage your career constructively and actively.

Further Reading

For a very interesting review of whether generation differences affect our career outlooks, see Parry, E (ed.) (2014) *Generational Diversity at Work*, New Research Perspectives. Abingdon: Routledge.

Think about the career and vocational tests introduced in this chapter and whether you would benefit from undertaking the self-review questionnaires. Many of these are licensed and so need to be paid for. Your careers adviser is the first place to visit to see if they can help.

3

Preparing for Work

Early Experience

A consistent theme in all our employer interviews has been developing early experience and showing passion for your proposed areas of work. Early experience helps you to ignite your passion for further study to achieve your ambitions. In later job interviews, early experience helps to focus attention on something to discuss during selection processes early experience will also demonstrate your readiness for work.

In Table 3.1 we give examples of how you can develop experience and understanding of your prospective areas of work. As well as developing experience, you will have the opportunity to develop contacts and networks for the future.

Remember, it is not simply turning up to these organisations but being able to explain, in covering letters and in interviews, how and why you are passionate about working in these fields. So be prepared to answer questions such as:

What did you do?

What did you enjoy?

What did you find more challenging?

How did you get on with other team members?

Competences

Understanding what is meant by 'competences' and being able to organise and articulate your competences in relation to organisation requirements are essential skills in employability. Therefore in this

TABLE 3.1   Ignite your passion by gaining work experience in your chosen areas

Here are some examples of the types of ways that you can gain early experience towards your chosen career.	
Aviation and Aeronautics	Royal Aeronautical Society (Young Person's Network) membership@ aerosociety.com
Charity	Start with local charity shops
	Volunteer at a hospice or with a local charity
Health, Social, Care and NHS	Excellent opportunities via your local hospitals and care centres and charitable organisations (Red Cross etc.)
	Check local hospices, many of whom have excellent schemes for volunteers
Media	Watch out for local events (e.g. BBC) requiring volunteers for the day/week
	Local radio stations (including university) may want assistants
	Charities often need media support and are worth contacting
	Offer to help run charity or organisation websites, social media or newsletters
Military	Local cadet units and university officer training units
	Reserve units also give valuable experience of whether the life is for you
Music	Local choirs and orchestras, National Youth Orchestra, National Youth choir
Teaching and Education	See if you can get experience in schools with after-school clubs, youth clubs, reading assistance etc.
	... and from our Employability Panel:
	I chose a university course which was a year less, which resulted in more time in the classroom from the beginning of the course.
	I had a Saturday job in a wedding shop before going to university and kept this going when I returned from uni for holidays.
	I approached a local head teacher and went into school to listen to children reading.
	I worked in local holiday club through the school holidays – all ages up to 11 (Mon.–Fri.).

section we summarise the theory behind competences and suggest a practical approach to enable you to manage the practical presentation of your own competences to an employer's requirements.

Whiddet and Hollyforde offer a useful working definition of competences:

> Behaviours that individuals demonstrate when undertaking job-relevant tasks effectively within an organisational context. (2003: 5–7)

Roberts (1997) distinguished between:

> Natural competencies – looking at personality factors such as extrovert/ introvert; emotional stability; agreeableness; conscientiousness; and open to variety of experience;

> Acquired competencies – knowledge and skill acquired at, or outside, work;

> Adapting competencies – how far an individual is able to adapt natural talents and skills to a new situation; and

> Performing competencies – observable behaviours and outcomes

Competences have continued to develop, and by 2003 Rees noted that there was no single definition; indeed, even the spelling of the term causes some debate. Even so, competences are in widespread use. For example, having researched 168 organisations, Suff (2010) found that 75.4 per cent of organisations believed that competences were vital to support organisational mission and objectives, but 30 per cent found using competences problematic. Of the organisational problems in using competences, Suff (2010) found problems in ensuring that users understood about how they worked and with line-management scepticism. Overall, these problems suggest less about doubts with competence frameworks themselves and more about their implementation. Even so, the 'employable' graduate must be familiar with competences and skilled in their practical application.

Well-prepared competences are of benefit to both the employee and the employer. When competences are written and designed with the organisation's vision and goals in mind they provide an opportunity for managers and employees to understand what behaviours and standards are required by the organisation. In the workplace typical examples of competences would include factors such as:

- team work
- customer service orientation
- problem solving

- delivering results
- managing with diversity and so on.

In the example in Table 3.2 we show generic types of competences which are often reviewed during selection and assessment. We have shown how, by using previous experiences, you can build up positive and developmental examples of your own competences.

This is a generic list. Before interview, check carefully that you can use this generic list to give examples – from the employer's own competence list – of how you meet the role requirements. In the list you are asked to show positive examples. Positive examples of competences are your best opportunity to show that you meet the job requirements. We also ask you to record development examples. Employers know that life isn't perfect – they want to see how you deal with setbacks and adversity. It is really important to think of examples where you can give a positive outlook to what you learned and why. If you managed to reverse a difficult situation, record that too. Prepare these examples in advance – don't get caught out with the worst thing that has happened to you and try to talk your way out of it. Employers look for learning, not dramatic impact.

We recommend that you develop a similar list. This will be for your own use. It will not be for showing potential employers. Instead, it will enable you to prepare thoroughly beforehand, and be in a much stronger position to manage during your interviews.

Time spent in preparing this list will be helpful for interacting with your CV and save you time trying to think of good examples during interviews. The development examples will be useful to develop your own individual learning plan for the future (see Chapter 5). During interview you may be asked to give examples of competences where things have gone wrong or where you have had lessons to learn. Use your development examples for this, but only use examples where you have successfully turned round a difficult situation – don't try to talk your way out of disasters!

When you discuss competence examples use 'I' not 'we' to describe what *you* have done.

It should be possible for you to come up with three to four good examples for each competence from your own student, intern, voluntary and vacation experience.

Once you are in a career role, keep this list up to date – at least every six months. That way, as role opportunities come up you will be more ready to submit a high-quality application in the short time before the final application date.

TABLE 3.2 Example of competence inventory

Competence	Positive examples	Development examples
Customer (working with internal or external customers)	Complimented for manner of dealing with awkward customer (or client, user, patient) complaint.	Find it hard at times to deal with aggressive customers who won't listen to reason, but recognise the need to listen to their needs and resolve them – show examples
Team (how successfully you work as part of a team; have a look at group styles in Chapter 6 to understand different roles within groups and teams)	Nominated as employee of the month by colleagues for team work. Seen as a person who comes up with different ideas and resource support. Concerned that group continues to focus on delivery of task.	Learned in a team exercise event whilst an intern that team needs to be balanced, with all views taken into account. Ensure that dominant voices do not swamp out ideas and concerns from the overall team (Be constructive about team experiences – do not attribute blame and failure to others. Show what happened, what you learned, and how you would do things differently another time)
Delivering results	Always relied on to deliver to required quality and time standards. Volunteered to stay late to ensure completion of major project. Sales, income, costs which you may have managed.	Examples of when you did not deliver what was required. What did you learn from this experience? How would you do it differently another time?
Self-organising (including work prioritisation)	Always seek to plan activities for the following 6 months. In work situations, seek clear agreed performance targets with line manager. Keep line manger up to date at an early stage if time, cost, quality or other performance targets are likely to be compromised .	Failed to achieve xxx because I didn't balance needs of all the stakeholders. Managed to recover this, but it has taught me to ensure that stakeholders' views are taken into account and update them on progress

(Continued)

TABLE 3.2 (Continued)

Competence	Positive examples	Development examples
Problem solving and using initiative	Asked to come up with some fresh ideas to address a particular issue. Discussed with colleagues and did some web searches to come up with some new approaches which were then accepted.	Made some assumptions without fully investigating and understanding all the relevant factors; learned to map and check with all stakeholders in future
Paying attention to diversity (how actively you ensure that everyone is treated fairly)	Show how you have been exposed to a variety of gender, age and ethnicity groups though voluntary work. Volunteered with local charity as a support worker for disabled visitors to outside broadcast etc.	
Leading others	Limited experience to date at work. Helped induct and act as buddy to new colleague. At university, organised society speakers. Sports captain – had to remove friend from team. Student peer mentor. Trained new staff members in vocation work.	Difficulties with particular team members? How did you sit down and resolve these and work together in the future?
Showing resilience (dealing with setbacks)	Needing to re-sit exams, which taught me that I should never give up, even though it threatened my first choice of university. Disappointed not to be selected for [job title], but asked about gaps and later was successful in selection. Your strong desire to get into this particular organisation, and how you have prepared for it in studies, work experience etc.	Be cautious about wearing your heart on your sleeve for this type of question. If you are asked about a setback which caused you particular problems, find one where you overcame the setback
Managing own learning	Keep my own learning plan If you do say something, make sure you can show it! See example in Chapter 5.	

Making the Most of Sources of Employment

To maximise your chances of finding the job that is right for you, you will need to make the most of the sources of employment available to you. In this section we examine what those sources may be, what our Employability Panel thought of them, and advice about how to maximise the use of the sources.

As you gain employment experience, in whatever capacity, ensure that you have contact details for the future of a person or office holder who can confirm your start and finish dates, and whether your employment has been satisfactory or, even better, give a reference if required.

Increasingly, employers seek to avoid litigation by not giving character references but only confirm employment dates. This is especially important if you are planning to develop your career in one of the many areas which requires pre-employment regulatory or security vetting and where a detailed record of your movements, often going back several years, may be required.

Starting dates can often be delayed for long periods when potential employers are unable to verify where you were and what you were doing, especially during gap periods overseas.

Using Careers Services

We asked our Employability Panel which methods they had found most useful in finding career work. The average (modal) results are shown in Table 3.3.

Careers services should be an early starting point in developing your employability. However, as you will see in Table 3.3, the

TABLE 3.3   Employability Panel: What were the most useful approaches in finding career employment? (N=50)

	Little/no use	Some use	Useful	Very useful
Careers services				
Employment fairs				
Employment agencies				
Networking				
Social media				
Other		Job adverts, including online		

majority view of our Employability Panel suggested this was the least useful support in finding career, although we should also say that a small number said the careers advice they received was excellent. We discussed these findings with a sample of university careers advisers. Their responses help us to discuss what to expect from the careers service and we hope that this will help you to make more effective use of this service. However, as we look at Table 3.3, bear in mind that really active searches would use all these opportunities to their maximum potential.

Despite the experiences of the Employability Panel in using these different sources, some of the weakest responses (e.g. use of careers services) came from poor use of the potential value rather than the intrinsic strengths or weaknesses of the resource itself. Therefore in this section we explain how to make the most of each employment resource. In Exhibit 3.1 we show what one of university careers advisers we interviewed offered in order to make the most of this resource.

Exhibit 3.1

Using University Careers Services

Brian Staines, Formerly Head of Careers Guidance at the University of Bristol, offers the following advice.

What types of service should a student look for from the careers service?

I would suggest that students actively start to think about the future, and to approach the Careers Service from their first year of study. This gives time to develop options, experiences, ideas and may mean rejecting early ideas which don't work out as they had expected.

Some students are crystal clear about what they want from their future careers. In this case the Careers Service can give access to employers, careers fairs, advice with CVs and interview techniques. In many ways, students who know what they want to do have a clearer pathway but can still benefit greatly in improving opportunities through the Careers Service.

Students who have less idea about their futures can be reassured – their position is not at all unusual. Here, the Careers Service can offer discussions and (where necessary) tests to distil some appropriate ideas on the future. But is has to be for the student to understand what they want and to take this forward; it is not for the Careers Service to push the student into a 'good' career, but to help them to understand what they want to do and help them get there – and if that means, for example, fulfilling an ambition to work in a fish canning factory in Norway, then so be it. The Careers Service may also offer appropriate psychometric testing to help the student, using tests such as Prospects Planner, but there are huge health warnings about the value of psychometrics and the value of their use in shaping careers choices.

I also encourage 'unsure' students to go along to employers' presentations to hear about opportunities – anything to increase awareness of the range of opportunities. And even if the employers' presentation turns out not for you – well, learn from the experience, eat the food and then go away!

From all this, the 'unsure' student is encouraged to develop a range of ideas and experiences through work experience, volunteering, travelling and so on.

What about after graduation?

Many universities will continue to offer services to their alumni for up to three years after graduation. Some will also support students – usually for a fee – who are now home but attended a different university for their degree studies. So if you need help, it is worth investigating this.

Employment Careers Fairs

It is easy to underestimate the value of careers fairs, and too often students fail to plan for careers fairs. As a result they arrive ill prepared and assume that they are at the fair simply to find out about possible job opportunities. But employers rarely invest time and resources in careers fairs simply to extend their brand names – they are there to start the process of finding new talent who can be progressed on to initial job screening. So to make the most of the career fairs:

- Find out about careers fairs at your own university and at universities local to yours or near home. (If you get into careers fairs at other than your own university, you may meet employers who do not visit your own university. Check beforehand that you can get in without a university-specific ticket.)
- Plan these dates into your diary.
- Prioritise which organisations you wish to see and what you hope to get from them. Don't simply drift around.
- Go looking presentable. It is not a formal job interview, but employers will be forming an opinion of you and whether they could see you fitting within their organisation.
- Engage with the employer representative and have a couple of questions prepared in advance.
- Take copies of your CV to leave with potentially interested employers.
- Find out about selection criteria and development opportunities.
- Get contact details (name, role, contact address) of access points if your own area of interest is not represented on the employer stand that day.

Sometimes you will make contacts at careers fairs which will lead to future recruitment opportunities. At other times there will not be a significant development other than to find that you do not want to work in that organisation after all. In both cases, however, you will develop a sense of what is required for your future area of employment and the criteria which prospective employers will use to assess new entrants.

Employment Agencies

Agencies may help you find career opportunities which are less 'obvious', and are especially useful in finding specialist careers such as marketing or logistics. A good agency, working with you in partnership to find work, may also help in finding you shorter-term work to develop your experience, and be candid with you in giving advice about your strengths and weaknesses and how to position yourself more positively in applications.

In the UK the fees for finding employees through an agency are met by the employer. *A very few agencies may try to charge the job applicant too – we do not recommend that you use agencies who charge a fee to the job seeker.*

In the Exhibit 3.2 we show the value of using an agency (in this case, LeapUK) that does work in partnership with graduate applicants to find appropriate roles and gives supportive feedback to potential job seekers.

Exhibit 3.2

Using Agencies and Application Tips – Allie Whelan, Director, LeapUK

Why would a graduate wish to seek work through an agency rather than finding work directly?

You need to do these things: network; apply directly to organisations; use agencies (befriend relevant agencies and consultants and develop a good relationship with them to make sure they know you and are fighting your corner).

I see this as prioritising your search in three ways:

1. Approach the top three organisations you want to work for.
2. Approach agencies that work with your preferred top three organisations.
3. Keep an eye on professional and trade journals, magazines and job boards.

As an employment specialist, what would you consider to be the most important factors in successful work applications?

In no particular order:

- Be bespoke for the role for which you are applying.
- Really focus your application on that role, rather than a generalised application. This usually means you need to tailor your CV for particular job roles.
- Really make your CV stand out – adapt it to what that employer is looking for.
- Apply the 'so what?' factor. With a CV or application you probably have about 20 seconds of the reader's attention, so:

  o make your application relevant to the job
  o make it relevant to your strengths (otherwise, don't waste your time)
  o avoid over-long and complicated covering letters.

- Be realistic about what you really want. Avoid being general and vague. Stick to your passions and learn to use your time wisely.
- Get experience. If at the moment you genuinely don't have what they are looking for, put yourself out into the market to get work experience – either in voluntary work or internships – to get the experience to use in interviews.
- Ask really good – brilliant – questions at interview.
- Prepare yourself thoroughly for the interview – know the organisation.

What are the most negative factors in not finding work?

- Lack of focus. Approach job hunting as a full-time job in its own right.
- Failure to use social media. Use LinkedIn, see what is being discussed, behave as if you are already in the role to which you aspire.
- Lack of attention to detail.
- Poor grammar and spelling in the application documents.

Good CV or good covering letter – which is more important?

Without doubt, a great CV. Your covering letter must be brief. Why are you the 'go to' person for this role?

Networking

It may be surprising that networking remains so important in finding a future role, especially as more structured advertising and selection processes are used to fill roles. Even so, our Employability Panel confirmed the finding of other studies that networking helps to find roles and better understand organisation requirements. At a more subtle level, it may also help you to tune in to the 'language and culture' of that organisation: this is likely to help with any future job applications, or may make you realise it is not for you.

Networking exposes you to wider job opportunities than you may find through conventional advertising. Furthermore, as people within your networks share information with you they are more likely to refer you opportunities where they feel there is some degree of fit – and so prospects of finding a suitable role.

It pays to be prepared for successful networking. Networking can start with family and friends as well as alumni who have joined organisations ahead of you. If you are attending a formal event (careers fair, work exchange or a conference) check the attendance list to find 'must see' people. When you do meet them, actively show an interest in what they are doing rather than spend the time telling them about yourself (this is more flattering to the person, and if they are interested in you they will ask you). Get their business cards and make sure you send them a LinkedIn invitation within 24 hours of the meeting.

Careers fairs are, of course, also a good opportunity to network, but don't kid yourself that you are looking around the stalls for interesting brochures. Employers will also be there to identify early talent, so go looking well prepared and well groomed, and take copies of your CV in case they are immediately interested. For careers fairs, make sure that you have read a bit about your target organisations before you go. Again, follow up with a LinkedIn invitation within 24 hours of meeting.

Once you are in work don't simply give colleagues who move on a good luck card, but stay in touch with them. Former colleagues may be asked for recommendations for new recruits in their new places of work, and it could be you. Even without job recommendations, social media will give you an idea of their experiences in other organisations, as will periodically meeting on a social basis.

Social Media

We have already seen the importance of good networking as a way of enhancing employability skills. Our Employability Panel also found this to be one of the most effective ways of finding out about career opportunism (see Table 3.3).

Social media is a critically important part of good networking, both as part of networking and as a way to showcase your own suitability for work. We asked Helen Hammond of Elephant Creative why job search candidates should use social media as a central part of their networking and job search strategy. Her guidance is shown in Exhibit 3.3.

Exhibit 3.3

Using LinkedIn to Get Your Dream Job

Helen Hammond of Elephant Creative explains why job search candidates should use social media as a central part of their networking and job search strategy.

Not only is LinkedIn the leading social media tool for Business to Business (B2B) communications, bar none, it looks set to grow yet further. Predictions for expansion in 2016 and beyond include a greater emphasis on published content, SlideShare integration and the inevitable commercial opportunities for organisations to promote their wares. But why should you care about all this, personally?

The last three jobs that I have recruited for, for clients, have been placed entirely via LinkedIn.

It's a fact. That's why. In the majority of cases I never even saw a separate CV and there weren't any job application forms. Everything was advertised, applied for, scored and assessed using individual LinkedIn profiles.

The reality is that it simply isn't possible to ignore LinkedIn and expect to get the top jobs any longer. A 2013 study by the Society for Human Resource Management found that 77 per cent of employers were using social networks to recruit, a sharp increase from the 56 per cent who reported doing so in 2011. And amongst the recruiters using social tools, 94 per cent said they were using LinkedIn. When the study was repeated in 2015, 87 per cent of HR professionals said it was either very or somewhat important for job seekers to have a social media presence on LinkedIn and that in 2015 alone nearly two-thirds of organisations (65 per cent) had hired new employees who were sourced through social media sites.

Ok, so that doesn't mean they're all recruiting exclusively on LinkedIn, but they are using it to identify targets, make approaches and, crucially, research and assess shortlisted applicants. And when you think about that, can you really afford to wave it away as hype and digital frivolity?

Getting ahead of the game on LinkedIn, however, isn't complicated but it does take methodical, hard work.

1. **Put in the time**: You need to understand that your LinkedIn profile is, for many recruiters, replacing the CV. It's time to think hard about the things you want to say and to put the effort in to saying them well. Plan the different sections out in advance and don't be tempted to skip over sections.
2. **Support your arguments:** LinkedIn offers a real opportunity that traditional CVs don't, in that you can support your claims with evidence. One of the best things to see, as a recruiter, is a suite of documents demonstrating ability, experience and approach. These might include examples of work, reviews or articles you've written.

(Continued)

(Continued)

3. **Don't forget the professional photo**: You need to note the word 'professional' here. I'm not interested in seeing the trout pout or your best holiday shot. I am looking for someone that looks professional and understands the importance of first impressions.

4. **Get others involved**: One of the best things about LinkedIn is the option to include recommendations. Don't be afraid to ask people for them. LinkedIn offers you the functionality to do this directly and to review recommendations before they go live. Importantly, try to demonstrate a consistent reputation for good work rather than just having recommendations for one role.

5. **Think about how people will find you**: You might be applying for a job directly from an advert but you'd be amazed how many recruiters use LinkedIn to speculatively search for possible candidates. When you are planning out each section, think about the key words you need to include to ensure that you come up in all the right searches.

6. **Include your contact details**: One of the most overlooked sections of the LinkedIn profile is the contact details section. Make it easy for people to contact you by phone and email.

7. **Don't forget your CV**: It might be tempting to think that your LinkedIn profile is going to replace your CV. I believe in a 'belt and braces' approach. Include a copy of your CV as a supporting document, so that those who want it can access it easily.

8. **Demonstrate that you're active**: Being positioned as attractive to potential employers isn't just about having a perfect profile, it's also about demonstrating day-to-day activity in the right areas. Make sure you're saying things regularly and showing that your expertise is current. That means commenting on articles in the press, sharing news and giving examples of projects that you're working on.

9. **Be proactive**: Sitting back and waiting for recruiters to find you is likely to be a slow process (unless you're really amazing). Once your profile is up to scratch you can use the job search function to set up alerts for suitable jobs, as well as doing research about potential employers.

10. **Engage**: At its heart, LinkedIn is about networking – and that means being brave enough to actually talk to people. Be bold. If you want to work in a certain organisation then find the right people (whether through searching for them directly or looking on company pages or in groups) and make contact. Similarly, keep an eye on the people who have looked at your profile. If you make contact remember to keep things clear, short and respectful. At the end of the day, if you show professionalism and respect, as well as a bit of initiative, most people will be impressed.

Job search

Finally, some advice on using the job-search section itself. LinkedIn offers you a wealth of ways to look for suitable jobs and, thanks to its cost-effective advertising and simple, direct application process, is becoming the go-to place for recruiters. There are a variety of ways to find out about suitable jobs:

1. A simple job search by key words and the advanced search by a whole load of options.
2. Jobs in your network – in places where you have connections or follow organisations.
3. Jobs you might be interested in – suggestions from LinkedIn that you can filter by location, organisation size and industry.
4. Following companies – so that their adverts show up in your news feed.

Best of all, it doesn't have to be a full-time job. You can save jobs to review later and set up email notifications for job searches. You can even take out a paid-for profile that will move your details up to being featured in applicant searches.

Internships and Placements

In this section we will look at some of the practicalities of placements – and if your course does not have a formal placement, then think about internships and related experience. In Exhibit 3.4 we share advice from careers advisers and employers on the value of getting started with internships and placements.

Estimates vary, but it is generally believed that at least 29–30 per cent of higher education students undertake some form of internship or placement, either as part of their course or during vacation periods. So important is the need for relevant work experience that some PhD programmes now require internship experience, recognising that not everyone will look for academic careers on completion.

Exhibit 3.4

Getting Started with Placements and Internships

Finding the right work is not just about going for 'the perfect role' but getting a start, establishing a track record and then adjusting from that to the path that is right for you.

(Continued)

(Continued)

Employers usually think the placement/intern student is great and may offer work after graduation. Students who have done internships and placements usually do better in their degrees and develop practice-orientated learning. **Dr Tilly Line, Senior Careers Consultant, Employability and Enrichment Team, University of the West of England**

Internships and placements are incredibly important. Even so, as aspiring internships and placements are arranged, there must be very clear learning aims which both the organisation and the intern can actually achieve. Both sides need to be clear about the boundaries, and especially that interns do not lose track of their studies and personal development.

Good internships can start from Year 10 in school; ideally, interns can then develop a relationship with the employer. This may include volunteering to increase employability or training and work as Health Care Assistants. Previous experience to the NHS really helps candidates to understand what it is like to work here, and shows the enormous range of opportunities we have. In these ways internships expand an understanding of the very wide range of potential future opportunities, help understand the trust's values and show long-term commitment.

Internships and placements are important, but we also offer other opportunities, such as work experience and volunteering. For potential clinicians we also offer competitive places to attend our taster days. **Jane Hadfield, Head of Learning & Development, Human Resource & Development Directorate, North Bristol NHS Trust**

In international aid and development work, we place a high premium on previous experience. When an international emergency occurs people will tend to run away from it, but at Tearfund our purpose is to run towards it. As such we cannot send inexperienced people. Therefore internships are crucial, especially since few academic programmes specifically prepare people for dangers and unpredictability of international aid and development work. Our internships prepare people for roles as aid practitioners as well as professional jobs such as Finance, Fundraisers, Human Resources and so on. Most international aid and development agencies have similar internship programmes but a few, such as Save the Children, are developing partnerships with universities to co-create qualifications designed as career paths for graduates wishing to specialise in international aid and development.

Our internships typically last 1–2 years. All our jobs are advertised internally and once internships are completed colleagues can apply for these roles. **Patrick Goh, Head of Global HR People & Organisation Development, Tearfund**

In summary, the key reasons that you should consider a placement are:

- It will give you an opportunity to gain practical experience of an area of work which you may later pursue – or find it is not right for you.
- You will extend your network of contacts – in itself, this is an important contribution to finding work.
- You will demonstrate to your future employer your interest – your passion – for this type of work.
- In job interviews you will be able to discuss your competences and relate these to your chosen area of work – you have a much better chance of 'speaking the same language' as your prospective employers.
- Placements often lead to job offers at graduation. Some employers use internships and placements as a replacement for Graduate Assessment and put you directly onto the graduate scheme, provided that you have performed well.
- Students who have placements tend to perform better in their final academic assessments than those without this experience (e.g. see Mandilaras, 2004; Neugebauer and Evans-Brain, 2009; Mendez and Rona, 2010).

Employers also see the value of placements. In addition to having the opportunity to see a potential employee before making a permanent job offer, organisations also claim that former placement students are more likely to stay in the organisation than graduates who are recruited through traditional methods. Table 3.4 shows the diverse examples of what employers look for in placements and the types of opportunities they can offer.

TABLE 3.4 Employers and placements (what employers are looking for)

Organisation type	More about requirements and opportunities
Public Sector Agency	70 per cent of roles available do not require a specific degree subject.
	Competences required: self-management, team work, literacy, numeracy, business awareness, problem solving, customer awareness.
Supermarket Chain	May take graduate employees from placements.
	Specialist degrees are only relevant for a minority of specialised areas.
	Competences required include: drive, energy, willingness to learn, great customer service orientation.
Financial Services	Any degree subject may be considered, but corporate and specialist banking areas require maths, economics or related disciplines.
	Competences required include: judgment, drive, influence, working in teams.
	Job offers may be made on the basis of placements.
	Top tip: Find out about the organisation before you apply.

(Continued)

TABLE 3.4   (Continued)

Organisation type	More about requirements and opportunities
International Voluntary Aid Organisation	Volunteering is hugely important in developing experience and ensuring you build the experience required for access, after graduation, to a role. It also helps ensure that it is the right area for you to work in on a longer-term basis.
International Investment Banking	Internships are the best way for candidates to finalise their decisions on their careers and where they want to begin it, and the best way for companies to ensure they are hiring the right people for them. The earlier you can secure an internship position (many are offered for first-year students now), the better – it demonstrates proactivity, commitment and hunger. Many internships lead to other internships and eventually full-time employment, so they are worth taking seriously.
Car Rental	Take about 80 per cent of graduates from internship programme. No degree specified. Use competences from full-time roles to assess suitability. Whilst on placement, will learn about sales, marketing, operations, customer services and business management. Time on internships counts towards management traineeship after graduation, so there is no need to start as a basic trainee.
NHS Trust	'These [internships and placements] are incredibly important. Even so, as aspiring internships and placements are arranged, there must be very clear learning aims, which both the organisation and the intern can actually achieve.' (Jane Hadfield, Head of Learning & Development, Human Resource & Development Directorate, North Bristol NHS Trust)
Global Communications	Any subject, but for commercial areas tend to look at business-related degrees. For specialist areas, relevant professional degree (computer sciences, HRM, engineering etc.). Focus on key competences, such as customer skills, teamwork, interpersonal skills, self-development, integrity.
Our tip	As well as looking at established internship and placement programmes, don't rule out applying to organisations directly to see if they have internship opportunities. Personalise your application. You will need a good covering letter, clear objectives and flexibility with dates. Find the name of a person to write to in the organisation, and don't simply write to 'Dear Sir or Madam'.

Source: Authors' research

You may not have the opportunity for a placement as part of your course. It is still worthwhile to see if you can get related experience through internships during your vacation, or even shorter-term experience. These will not give you the scope of benefits of placements, but they are still of value.

Be an Entrepreneur!

Working in a salaried role for an organisation may not suit everyone, and an increasing number of working age people prefer to set up their own business.

Being your own entrepreneur is outside the scope of this book, but we wanted to show that it may be a natural outcome for some. Entrepreneurs will usually have:

- a driving passion and belief in what they want to do
- clear focus
- the ability to work on their own as well as with other people
- considerable resilience
- somewhere to work (many successful businesses have, literally, started on the kitchen table)
- start-up capital and the ability to manage cash flow (lack of cash is often the death of business ideas)
- the ability to manage 'the business' as well as the great entrepreneurial idea.

There are many business start-up agencies and incubators to help new small businesses, and some university courses are specifically aimed at developing entrepreneurial skills. There is no single route to being successful as an entrepreneur. We have examples of people who started their own business immediately on graduation (and may have even been developing it whilst studying), to those who took full-time work first and worked on their own or with partners in their spare time to set up their business.

We asked Ed Schofield to tell us more about his journey to setting up his own business, and this is shown in Exhibit 3.5. There is no single journey to a business start-up but Ed's experience, the help he got and the challenges he faced are typical of the ups and downs encountered in running your own business.

Exhibit 3.5

Setting up as an entrepreneur
Ed Schofield and Schofield Trading

Whether entering employment or setting up in your own business, we have seen that passion and resilience are critical in developing employability. In this case study, we hear how one graduate overcame setbacks, first to gain relevant work experience and then to set up as an entrepreneur in his chosen field.

(Continued)

(Continued)

Having completed an Honours degree in Fine Art at the University for the Creative Arts, I worked towards a career as an artist and curator. This was what we were sold as the logical progression by our tutors, and why not? It became very obvious very quickly that this was not going to automatically bring in any income. I found on leaving university that the idealistic world described by our tutors and our place in it as new art graduates was misleading, and there was no suggestion of the reality that would come very quickly. Thinking back to what we were told about the potential open to us as prospective students before we enrolled and to our lectures about working as artists after university, it was in my view fraudulent at best. But it's easy to say that now.

I found it no problem finding work as a student to pay for my tuition. But after graduating, having tried to find a job stacking shelves to support myself whilst pursuing this 'idea' of becoming an artist, I found it impossible to find any work. The problem being that I was over-qualified. I found myself in a catch-22, no experience in any related workplace and too many qualifications to find an interim job.

The answer came in the form of unpaid work for 9 months with the Portland Quarry and Sculpture Trust, writing bids for funding, meeting with artists, helping geologists with stone carving and ultimately curating an exhibition of art, fossils, history and geology. This was an attractive prospect for a reporter, and ITV made a short documentary about my efforts. The key thing I learned from this is that, unlike our university's projected expectations, in the real world there is no place for art unless of course you have no need for an income. This was at the time of huge cuts to national arts funding, with centres and galleries closing left, right and centre. I did, however, take a lot away from this experience aside from the geological knowledge, in terms of integrity to a project. I learned that long-term vision is better than making a quick buck, and remaining focused on this long-term goal would indeed help to steer through difficult decisions.

Using this as a springboard (and in very need of money by now) I found a sculpture park in Surrey. They weren't advertising for staff but I walked in and asked for a job. I started off sanding wood and digging holes for sculptures to be installed, but before long I found myself at Sotheby's installing the sculpture we were selling, setting up a garden at Chelsea flower show and much more besides. I was then promoted into the company's interior design showroom, focusing on luxury interiors.

Here I found a very useful set of skills. Selling, buying, customer service and the logistics of running a small business on a daily basis. But what struck me the most was the limitations of it, the expectation that you would join a small company and stay for 10+ years with no real prospect of progression or development. Being expected to complete your duties and any others thrown your way day after day with no involvement or interest beyond the sale. As I'm sure with most businesses the bottom line is final, but as I have already explained the

FIGURE 3.1   Schofield Trading Co. logo

vision and ambition is, I think, more important. I did not feel there was any vision or chance of me achieving my ambitions, and this frustrated me. Wanting to achieve more than just make my boss richer. So I quit.

After four years of working for this company I decided to go it alone. In November 2014 I left the company and set up the Schofield Trading Company (see Figure 3.1) selling art, curios, sculpture, fossils and anything unusual I could find. I decided to do this as an online business (www.schofieldtrading.com) due to the global reach and comparative low cost. I approached the Prince's Trust for training and support, and was granted 'Prince's Trust Supported Status' in August 2015. The challenge has not been finding things to buy, but cash flow. I think any business will tell you this.

The Prince's Trust has helped me to structure my business, organise and structure a cash flow and how to organise the fundamental day-to-day financial running of a business; I would say that without this support and ongoing support from my mentor I would not have been as successful as I have been. Working in a business and running a business are two very different things. The demands you face every day to make the bill payments are a constant burden. However, the benefits far outweigh this. Your time is your own, your interests inspire you and your fascination within a subject makes your work feel like a hobby. It allows me to do what I want to do. In short, working for myself is complete freedom.

My long-term goal is to grow my business. My vision for the business is to be the top online retailer for unique and obscure items of note, selling the most interesting and desirable items on the market. In doing so I would hope to build up a substantial knowledge base on artefacts and art pieces. This in time will lead me to do a master's degree.

(Continued)

(Continued)

In conclusion I think that university is fundamentally a good thing, but you need to study for your own self-development, not employability (at least that's what I have found). I personally think I would have benefited from some of the real world before going into full-time higher education as it gives a perspective on what it is being told and what you expect as an outcome.

I cannot speak for all courses, but from my experience and seeing my friends graduate there seems to be a large reality gap between university and working in the real world. But if universities are behaving as businesses and selling employability via self-betterment as a commodity, it would be detrimental and not in their own interests to highlight the contradictions in their sales pitch.

Additional Support – Graduates and Students with Disabilities

So far we have seen that graduate employment is highly competitive. Graduates and job candidates with disabilities and underlying longer-term health issues may find additional challenges despite the legal requirement (in the UK through the Equality Act 2010) not to discriminate on the grounds of disability.

Specialist support for job seekers with disabilities is usually available from university careers services, and you should make early contact with your careers services (first year of studies is not too early, especially for arranging internships and placements) to make full use of the resources available. In addition, there are many specialist websites which can offer support, advice and opportunities: a representative sample is shown in the further reading section at the end of this chapter.

Conclusion

In this chapter we have discussed the breadth and depth of the preparations which we recommend to you in preparing for work. It's a long list, but not an impossible one. If you can do this effectively you are well on the way to building your employability portfolio. Do remember that although getting the experience is important, it is equally important to make sure that you record the experience so that you are able to explain in future applications how it is relevant for your application.

```
┌────────┤ ACTION ├────────────────────────────────┐
```

ACTION

Having read this chapter, we suggest that you think about the following action points:

- In looking for placements, don't only look at formal schemes – approach organisations which catch your imagination.
- When writing to an organisation about a potential placement or work experience, be clear about what you can offer the organisation, but also be clear about your objectives in requesting a placement.
- Keep your CV up to date.
- Keep examples of your competences up to date.
- As you complete working experience, ask for a contact who is prepared to verify your working dates (and possibly provide a work reference) in the future. This is especially important for overseas work.
- Be thoroughly prepared for and practise interviews, especially as you get closer to final selection.

Further Reading

There are several websites which have graduate opportunities, but also give candidate views of the selections procedures and experiences and what it is actually like to work for that organisation (e.g. see www.thejobcrowd.com/top-companies-to-work-for).

For information and advice on internships and placements, see Neugebauer, J and Evans-Brain, J (2009) *Making the Most of Your Placement*. London: SAGE.

For students with disabilities or underlying health issues there are many organisations which can help, including with offering placements with blue chip organisations, scholarships, advice and information and employer partnership events. For example, see:

EmployAbility at www.employ-ability.org.uk/

usemyability at http://usemyability.com/index.php?p=2

Disability Rights UK at www.disabilityrightsuk.org/careers-and-work-disabled-people

Scope at www.scope.org.uk/corporate-partnerships/our-partners

Blind In Business (for blind or partially sighted candidates) at www.blindinbusiness.org.uk/

Other organisations, such as the Business Disability Forum (at http://businessdisabilityforum.org.uk/) give an idea of the scope of activities which employers are undertaking to support job candidates with disabilities.

Look at the opportunities for placements and internships. There are many organisations out there to support you, including:

AIESEC: international opportunities, www.aiesec.co.uk/students/

Go Wales: work and placement experience across Europe, www.gowales.co.uk/

International Association for the Exchange of Students for Technical Experience (IAESTE): an independent, non-profit and non-political student exchange organisation providing students in technical degrees (primarily Science, Engineering and the applied arts) with paid, course-related training abroad and employers with highly-skilled, highly-motivated trainees, www.iaeste.org/

Mountbatten Scholarships: one-year paid internship in London or New York, www.mountbatten.org/

Prospects UK: internships, placements and postgraduate study opportunities, www.prospects.ac.uk/

RateMyPlacement: lively site with placement and work opportunities and employer ratings, www.ratemyplacement.co.uk/

STEP: organiser of paid student work placements and graduate internships, www.step.org.uk/

United Euro Bridge: a small UK-based non-profit organisation promoting work placements, self-employment and supports micro, small and medium businesses across Europe, http://unitedeurobridge.eu/new_site/

The small print: These sites are shown for illustration only. We feel they will be of interest to a wide range of students. We are not endorsing them. Check any site's conditions of use carefully. You should be able to find placement opportunities without paying any fees to an intermediate agency.

4

Finding Work

'I am a psychology graduate

What is the hardest thing about being a psychologist?

Finding a job'

(Debra Barraud, Humans of Amsterdam, Foto
Exhibition Openbare Bibliotheek Amsterdam, 2015.
Used with Permission.)

Introduction and Preparing for Applications

Preparing work application is a massively time-consuming process. There are very few shortcuts in the process. In this chapter we recommend how to prepare yourself for this process. With the number of graduates applying for roles, applications will receive only a very short period of consideration: those which have obvious gaps in background, competences, appropriate qualification or which contain gaffs and errors (see below) will be quickly discarded. If you cannot submit a well-prepared application, it is usually best not to waste your time. Here we present some tips for creating good applications.

Be Organised, and Get Organised Early

Being well organised throughout the process is important: it will help you to make the most of individual applications, and help when there are time pressures on application dates.

Make sure that you check the application deadlines of the employers you are most interested in. Your target employer(s) may have deadlines in the first term of your final year, so check, plan and prepare in the summer before your final year.

To be organised, you need:

- A generic CV with all your personal work history details on it. The generic CV is your 'library copy'. You would not send it to an employer but instead edit it down to the two sides which are most appropriate for that application. We cover CV preparation in more detail in the following section, 'Smart CVs'.
- A list of competence examples. See Table 3.2 for details about how to summarise examples of your competences. Again, this is a library copy for your personal use: you will take examples from this list to illustrate your suitability for the role for which you are applying. Your own list of competences, kept up to date throughout your career, will also enable you to attend job interviews and discuss positive examples of how you meet the job requirements.
- Sufficient time to understand what is required in the application; answer all the questions; and ensure that spelling and grammar are correct.

Here are some examples of the most common gaffs in job applications. Despite having spent time in the application, these gaffs ensure that your application is immediately discarded:

- spelling errors
- applying for unsuitable jobs
- poor grammar
- failing to read the job requirements and linking your background to the job requirements
- failing to answer all the employers' questions
- rushing to use a previous generic application – and showing your commitment to a competitor organisation!

Most importantly: When you have finished your application, ask a friend or family member to check it for you.

Demonstrate Your Passion for the Role for which You Are Applying

In preparing this book, every employer we spoke to and every placement agency emphasised the need to show your passion for the role being advertised. How does the role fit with what you have done already? How does the role fit with your longer-term plans? What immediate contribution can you make to the organisation? Check the employers' websites to see how you can align your skills with their needs.

Write a Convincing Covering Letter

It is useful to have a high-quality covering letter ready and amendable for each application. The covering letter may be:

- used as the covering letter for which it was intended
- to copy into application forms where you are invited to 'tell us in your own words' why you are suitable for the job
- useful to edit as a top four lines for a personal summary in your CV.

Not all employers require a covering letter, and the evidence is mixed as to whether this makes a big difference or no difference at all (with some employers preferring to rely on the application form or the CV). Typically, your covering letter will be:

- one side maximum, therefore clear and concise
- businesslike but not too formal, nor over-familiar
- a summary with evidence and short examples of how you meet the job requirements
- a demonstration of your passion for the organisation's objectives (without being creepily sycophantic!)
- typed, perfectly set out and free of grammar and spelling errors.

A sample covering letter is shown at Appendix C.

Be Ready for the Next Steps

Keep a copy of your application and the job description to hand so that you are ready when a reply comes in. Some organisations will reply quickly, others will feel like black holes. Be especially ready for unexpected phone calls, which may be to do a quick check on your application details, pre-screen you or invite you for interview. In particular, if you answer the phone from a number you don't recognise, make sure you answer it in a businesslike manner: it may just be that call you have been waiting for.

Smart CVs

Your CV is your core document for applications. Even if you apply online, your CV will be the document that informs most of the content of your online application.

There are many sources of advice and help for getting your CV right. In this section we suggest the best way to organise yourself to have a smart CV – one that you can tailor quickly and effectively to specific roles.

Much of the advice on CV preparation suggests, correctly, that a CV of more than two sides will not be read as carefully as a shorter CV. So the CV you submit needs to be two sides. However, different roles will require different emphases on your suitability and experience, and two sides are unlikely to be sufficient to cover this. Therefore we suggest you organise your CV as follows:

- First, to have a generic CV, which covers all your experience to date, wherever you are in your career. This generic version can be several pages long.
- Second, you use the generic CV to edit your pitch in a smart CV – one that is tailored and specific for the post for which you are applying .

Your smart CV is the CV tailored by you from the generic CV to show how you are the most suitable person for this specific role. Link what you say to the role requirements. The smart CV should contain:

Short personal profile of 4–5 lines: This links your key skills and passion to work in that role for that employer. You may have one or two generic models, but this statement needs to be tailored to each role you apply for.

Summary of education: As with career history, show first your most recent qualifications (or studies towards an imminent qualification). Don't bend the truth – this is the first thing you will be found out on. Emphasise qualifications and distinctions, and play down grades if you were not so good at some stages of your education. GCSE grades don't need to be shown, but make sure that successes in Maths and English are shown.

Career history: In reverse chronological order, with the most recent roles first. For each role show: the employer; dates in role; job title; key aspects of the role; key achievements in the role (use 'I' not 'we' to show your contribution to the achievements. Practise 'I' not 'we' for job interviews, as employers want to understand *your* contribution, not what the team did). This section needs to be accurate, pithy and relevant to the job.

Competences and skills summary: In the section on 'Competencies' in Chapter 3, we explain competences and skills. Employers still place a big emphasis on transferable skills. See what competences are required for the role you are applying for (which should be on the job or role specification or description) and tailor your answers accordingly. You may not have enough space for competences in your CV: if not, summarise them in the covering letter you write or, if you are applying online, use them to amplify your application in the box for 'additional information' or 'tell us more about why you consider yourself suitable for this role'.

Additional training and skills: Show that you have a breadth of interests and experience, from lifeguarding to cashing up the shop/bar at the end of the day, to a Duke of Edinburgh's award and so on . For almost any job for which you apply, don't forget to show your IT skills. For more specialist roles, say which software you have used. Show also your language skills, with an honest assessment of your capability (basic, good, conversational, fluent and bilingual).

Additional Posts of Responsibility

Pastimes: include three or four, but do not include 'socialising' as a hobby or pastime. Some advisers doubt the value of including pastimes. We disagree. Showing, briefly, that you have a range of interests shows a well-rounded candidate. A further advantage for applicants is that interviewers may pick up on their shared interest in your hobbies and sports – it helps to develop relationships during selection stages.

Don't bother with: referees' names and addresses (they'll get them if they are interested, but ensure that you have three referees lined up – you will usually need two); photographs (in the UK); fancy layout and design using software packages (use Word, set it out well, use narrow margins but don't overcrowd the page).

The order of your smart CV will probably be as shown in the above checklist, but there are variations. For example, if you have a high level of work experience, your personal statement may say 'Graduate with substantial experience in ...', with your work experience shown first and qualification further down the list.

We strongly recommend that you have a careers adviser, friend or family member check your smart CV for comprehensiveness and to check spellings and grammar (the most common reasons to reject CVs outright). Don't forget to have a two-sided CV with your LinkedIn page (see Exhibit 3.3).

CVs are an art, not a science. There are good practices, but the best CVs are the ones which most appeal to the person who receives them. The most challenging part of the CV is getting started. In Appendix B we show a typical CV, with annotated comments to get you started. Linked with your CV, Appendix C shows a sample covering letter.

What You Can Expect in Selection and Assessment

Employers want to process applications as quickly and cost effectively as possible. In the early stages of selection you may find that you have little direct contact with the organisation. Here we discuss the types of selection procedures you may encounter. We look at how to succeed, but we also look at how to fail by considering some of the most common mistakes which are made at each stage.

Telephone Interviews

Some organisations will use initial telephone screening to check whether you are worth bringing to further interview. You may be given advance notice of a telephone interview. Sometimes there will be little notice of a telephone interview, especially where organisations are running assessment centres and realise there are not a sufficient number of candidates attending. Provided that you have done the necessary preparation, it should not be difficult to pass an initial telephone interview, but you need to be ready at short notice. See Table 4.1 for a summary.

Your minimum aim: To pass

TABLE 4.1   Succeeding and failing in telephone (and video) interviews

How to fail	How to pass	How to excel	Preparation and practice
Get caught on the hop and unprepared. Organisations may call you at short notice to ask you questions about your application	Be prepared so that you have your personal information and application ready and accessible at short notice, and can deal with 'unexpected' phone calls	If you are given advance notice, treat the interview as a business meeting – have a quiet place for the call, get ready about 15–30 minutes beforehand; some candidates also feel more confident if they are standing up during the discussion	Make sure you have information about the organisation and have your application to hand

Numeracy, Oral and Spatial Reasoning Tests

Many organisations use online tests in numeracy, verbal skills or spatial reasoning for initial candidate screening. Most graduates should have the ability to do these tests, but the main reasons for failing are often being rusty, understanding the 'rules' of the tests too slowly, and failing to finish enough questions on time.

If you have not undertaken these tests recently it will help you to practise. It is especially important to get into the right tempo for doing these tests, which are usually timed. You may be able to answer a few of the questions by glancing at the tests without time pressures, but it is much more challenging to do a battery of tests under live conditions. So do practise!

Websites such as http://cebglobal.com/shldirect/index.php/en/practice-tests offer useful practice sessions. Practise on these sites before you start the selection processes, and practise again when you have been told that you will be undertaking these types of tests.

Your aim is to show that you have these basic skills, so passing is usually enough. See Table 4.2 for a summary.

Your minimum aim: To pass

TABLE 4.2   Succeeding and failing in numeracy, or verbal, spatial reasoning communication

How to fail	How to pass	How to excel	Preparation and practice
Assume that you will be OK on the day – don't practise	Spend a few hours on practice sessions, and repeat this shortly before you do the online tests or attend an assessment centre	Not usually necessary though some roles may require high levels of personal fitness, hand–eye coordination or excellent results in mental agility tests	Spend time with online test and practice sessions

Don't be put off by these tests – treat them as enjoyable challenges |
| | Stay focused during the tests. Keep an eye on time. Move on to the next question if you are stuck and the tests allows you to move on | Consider whether you are going into a specialist field where these types of tests will be more critical to your success in the selection process. Find out what is required in advance and practise | |

Interviews

Whilst you may be able to afford to be good (rather than excellent) in many of the selection methods used so far, you need to excel during face-to-face interviews. In part these are about checking your ability, experience and commitment. But they are also about making an assessment: Is this the type of person we want working here? Is this someone I would wish to work with? Do this candidate's values fit with the values of the organisation?

You can expect two types of interview, structured and unstructured. You need to be ready for both.

In **structured interviews**, all candidates will be asked the same or very similar questions. Typically these will be based on job competences, and you will be asked to show how your competences meet – or exceed – the competences of the role for which you are applying. Structured interviews often begin with a simple question such as 'Tell me a bit about yourself.'

Structured interviews need quite a bit of preparation if you are going to show yourself at your best. Prepare yourself for the most typical questions you may be asked (see Exhibit 4.3), and practise giving these answers with a friend or mentor. You can prepare by completing the competence inventory, which is shown in Table 3.2.

For **unstructured interviews** it is less easy to prepare and less easy for you to manage during the interview. The interviewers themselves may be highly skilled at unstructured interviews. On some occasions, and more difficult for you to manage as a candidate, the interviewers may not be fully prepared to see you, may lack training in selection interviewing, or feel that they have some special insight (often erroneously) in how to pick a successful future employee.

Unstructured interviews are more difficult to prepare for, but there are still some things which you can do. First, share interview experiences with your friends and see what kind of questions they have had to deal with. For example, if you were asked 'If you were an animal, what kind of animal would you be?', think about what kind of answer you would give and the reasons for your choice. Unstructured interviews may also push your patience to the limits (in some cases that is intentional): stay calm.

Whether you find yourself in a structured or unstructured interview, be true to yourself and to your values. It should go without saying that you need to keep your cool as well; especially in unstructured interviews, bear in mind that interviewers may be looking to see how you react when pushed to the limits. State your points clearly, but don't rise to the bait of a contrived argument and debate which becomes emotional. See Table 4.3 for a summary.

Your minimum aim: To excel

Group Exercises, Role Plays and Presentations

Group exercises and role plays may be used to see how you may operate in real-life situations. Group exercises can be difficult (and quite subjective) for recruiters to assess. So a good tip is to make your mark against the criteria which will enable you to 'pass' (see below), rather than stand out as a candidate for good or not-so-good reasons. See Table 4.4 for a summary.

TABLE 4.3   Interviews

How to fail	How to pass and excel
Don't read the job details	Make a strong start.
	Be ready with a 60-second summary about yourself.
Don't align your experience and skills with the job requirements	Be ready with your CV and competence examples (see Exhibit 4.3, Typical questions asked during structured interviews).
Treat it as another interview	Check the job details and organisation details carefully.
	Show passion – and if you can show genuine passion, even better!
	Practise direct eye contact with a range of interviewers.
	Be ready with great questions.
Lying. Mark Twain is reported to have written that 'if you tell the truth, you don't have to remember anything'. Anywhere in the selection process, lying is a sure way to fail. It may take a while for your deceit to be uncovered, but in the end, the system is likely to catch up with you: you may even lose your job as a result of it	Position your experience assertively and confidently. Don't lie about your actual or expected degree class, nor your previous experience. If you have unspent criminal convictions (or spent convictions but are applying for roles where you cannot claim exemption from disclosure), make sure that you declare them and that you can articulate what you have learned from the experience.

Your minimum aim: To pass (although in some selection processes such as for leadership roles you will need to excel)

TABLE 4.4   Succeeding and failing in role plays

How to fail	How to pass	How to excel	Preparation and practice
Feel a bit lost on the day – not sure what the topic is, be disorientated by the exercise	Know that you will need to make 3–4 really good interventions in the session – make sure that you do	For specialist roles where leadership is a key requirement, you may need to excel rather than pass. Check this in advance	You need to practise these skills in advance. How do you do in society or tutorial meetings?

Discuss with friends going through similar selections, and give feedback to each other |

(Continued)

TABLE 4.4 (Continued)

How to fail	How to pass	How to excel	Preparation and practice
Say nothing Say 'I agree with that' (without adding to the conversation) Say too much: dominate the conversation and block out other team members	As well as making your contributions, be a good team player – keep an eye on timing for the group; if members are quiet, say 'I'd like to hear X's view on this point'; when the discussion has progressed, use phrases to summarise the group position, e.g. 'so to summarise, are we saying …'		Demystify the process by finding out more about group dynamics. Read: Tuckman, 1965 (Group working dynamics) Belbin, 1981 (Working Style in Groups) Janis, 1971 (Group Thinking) See Chapter 6 for further details
Think that the assessors want to watch a run-through of *The Apprentice* – instead, they are looking for people who can listen to others, keep an eye on group progress and timing, come up with good ideas and act as good team members	Have these objectives clearly in mind and make sure that you make your mark		

Presentations

A pre-prepared presentation, or an unprepared presentation, is a regular feature of assessments centres. Assessors will tend to have a stronger positive impression of a candidate whom they have seen present well. See Table 4.5 for a summary.

Your minimum aim: At least good, and preferably to excel

What Can Go Wrong – with Your Assessors

Having looked at assessment processes, we now look at what can go wrong with your assessors, and with you, during the process. Selection processes are notoriously difficult for predicting future role suitability.

TABLE 4.5   Succeeding and failing in presentations

How to fail	How to pass	How to excel	Preparation and Practice
Don't prepare. As authors, we have know times when even though candidates are given advance notice of the need to present, and the topic, they may come unprepared on the basis of being 'too busy'. They usually fail, as this also suggests poor work prioritisation	If you have been given the presentation title in advance, practise, especially with content, timing and dealing with questions	Engage your audience: • Maintain scanning eye contact with the audience • Inject some originality in content or style – but avoid being quirky	Make and take opportunities to present: e.g. in seminars (even if – perhaps especially if – these are the least comfortable environments for you, they enable you to develop your techniques), club and society meetings etc.
Tell yourself that you are not good in presentations. Instead, take time in your studies to get as much experience and good technique as possible	Use good presentation skills during this assessment. They do not come without practice and technique, so prepare this in advance	Be a bit different – but don't be a clown	Use a formula for every presentation: 1. Title 2. Aims 3. Content 4. [Recommendations where appropriate] 5. Conclusion
Learn to 'rise above' your nerves and tension – we are all tense in presentations – the issue is controlling nerves	Take control of your presentation environment. Arrive in good time and set the room – or at least the presentation position – to how you want it and how you feel comfortable		Envisage yourself doing a great presentation – and then deliver it!

Even in more structured selection interviews, assessors make mistakes and errors of judgment. These have been called 'unconscious bias' – either making an over-flattering assessment of a candidate or finding an early fault in a candidate which then impairs further objective assessment of the candidate.

Many of the recruitment and assessment techniques used by organisations have been challenged for their effectiveness in picking the best candidate. So if you have not succeeded in an assessment centre or other type of selection test it might be you – but then again, you can take comfort that the assessors may have made an error of judgment too. Mistakes electors make during interviews are shown in Exhibit 4.1. The challenge for you, however, is to ensure that the same mistakes are not repeated!

Exhibit 4.1

Mistakes Selectors May Make in Interviews

Selective attention: Interviewer only considers selected information and data, rather than looking at all information available on a candidature. As a result selectors may decide that a candidate is 'suitable' or 'unsuitable' in the first few minutes of the interview, and spend the rest of the meeting finding information to confirm the original decision.

Halo effects: Interviewer draws conclusions on the basis of only one criterion (e.g. intelligence or appearance) and interprets all other interview data in the same positive way irrespective of how positive or negative that data is.

Contrast effects: Interviewers may look at a fairly strong performer in the interviewee and consider that candidate to be much stronger than in reality because the interviewer has just seen a much weaker candidate.

Projection: Interviewer assumes other people 'are like us', (e.g. conscientious) and makes an error of judgment as a result.

Stereotype: Interviewer does not look at the individual attributes of a particular candidate but judges the candidate based on the perception of the characteristics of the group in which they are classified or stereotyped (e.g. too old, too young, immigrant, well brought-up, elite university, lesser ranked university etc.).

Heuristics: Interviewer tries to simplify complex decisions by taking shortcut judgments.

Source: based on Newell and Shackleton, 2001

Exhibit 4.2

Uncovered lies in the selection process

Even people who should know better still get found out. Here is a sample from professional people who got caught – and what happened to them.

NHS HR manager who lied on her CV and was given a six-month suspended prison sentence and ordered to pay £9,600 in compensation. The employee falsely claimed that she held a degree in Human Resource Management and said she was part way through a Chartered Institute of Personnel and Development course. She had been working as an HR manager for six years.

Barrister dismissed for falsely claiming degrees from Harvard and Oxford.

New Zealand Defence Force's chief scientist failed to declare a job he had been fired from the previous year for incompetence. Failing to spot this and errors in the CV were described as 'seriously embarrassing' (Sands, 2010). The chief scientist was dismissed.

Nurse manager sacked and given a suspended prison sentence after falsely claiming a degree (she had dropped out of university) and forging documents.

According to an article in *The Guardian* (Rowley, 2014), the Higher Education Degree Datacheck reports that about one-third of graduates misrepresent their degree class or results, even though this is so easy to check. The national press also report that graduates misrepresent the subjects they have studied in order to submit job applications.

Exhibit 4.3

Typical questions asked during structured interviews

These questions, and the answers, may seem predictable. Candidates often fail on the easiest questions, so make sure you are genuinely ready.

'I've read your CV, but tell me a bit about yourself, in your own words.' (Limit your answer to one minute, maximum.)

'Why have you applied to us?' (Research the organisation and show how you can make a difference to them. Be enthusiastic! Avoid over-long answers on what you think you can get from working for that organisation.)

'Which other organisations have you applied to?' (Only mention a couple, and only where the role is very similar to the one you have applied for; make clear your preference for this organisation.)

'Give me an example of when you demonstrated the competence of …' (To answer this type of question – and you will probably have many questions framed in this way – you must have pre-prepared examples of competences based on your earlier experiences. See Chapter 3 on competences.)

'Give me an example of when you have failed to demonstrate the competence of …' or 'What has been your greatest disappointment?' (Again, use

(Continued)

81

(Continued)

your pre-prepared competences to answer this question. Use examples where you have turned round a difficult situation and succeeded, or learned a deeper lesson for the future. Do not use the worst-case example you have – the assessors are looking for resilience and learning.)

'What would you like to ask us?' (Use this opportunity to get further information, but also impress the assessors. See the next section on 'Killer questions to ask'.)

Killer Questions to Ask in Interviews

Often you will be asked for any questions you have about the organisation or the proposed role. This is an opportunity to find out more information about the organisation. But if you handle it appropriately, it may be an additional opportunity to impress the assessors.

As with answers to your interview questions, the questions you ask of the interviewers should be prepared in advance. The questions you ask can also be a chance for you to show again your passion and interest in the organisation.

'I've read [make sure you have!] and heard a lot about the organisation's main goals and objectives looking forward, but I would be interested to hear your own views on what you think is important.'

Asking this question may give you additional insight into the organisation. Seeing how the interviewers handle the question may also give you some idea of the culture within the organisation. Also some interviewers will be impressed with your question.

'What happened to the previous person [or graduate intake cohort] and how and why did they move on?'

You will usually get a stock answer, but it shows you are interested.

'I really want to focus on my learning and development over the next couple of years. Can you tell me how this will be supported?'

Again, this shows that you want to progress, but without directly asking when you can expect your first promotion. The answer given, as well as being of value in helping you decide whether to join them, will also give you an idea of the culture of the organisation, particularly whether they want to develop you and how they would do this.

'Looking forward three to five years, where would you reasonably expect someone for this year's intake to be?'

This shows you focus on the longer term, but may also show that you have not read the recruitment literature properly, so make sure you do read it before you use this question.

'What attracted you to join the organisation and how has this developed in practice?'

Answers will help you judge the organisation and may help you connect further with the interviewer.

Questions to avoid include detail on the contract of employment, which you can sort out and negotiate once you have been offered a role, when you will be in a much stronger position to negotiate. Similarly, do not ask when you will hear more about your application (they usually tell you this in the interview wrap up), so don't waste a question on it unless they fail to tell you at the end.

Assessment Centres

Assessment centres are expensive and time-consuming for employers to run, but well-structured assessment centres are regarded as having the best predictor of future job success. Even so, their predictive values of finding the best person for the job varies between 0.41 and 0.66 (see e.g. Pilbeam and Corbridge, 2006: 173).

Assessment centres will usually incorporate: structured (and possibly unstructured) interviews; presentations; psychometric exercises; role play and group exercises; and some form of work simulation.

In practice, if your assessment centre simulates the workplace or work events, both you and the employer will have a good idea about future success. If you feel you are not ready for the assessment centre, then you may need to prepare yourself better or practise further.

As an example of what you may expect from less conventional assessment centres, Virgin Money won the CIPD 2015 Award for Best Recruitment and Talent Management Initiative with assessments that included a half-time talk to an England football team, talk to an unresponsive bouncer, and getting through a smoke-filled room. Virgin Media focused on activities which were not competence based (in their terms), but difficult to prepare for. No doubt Virgin Money had their reasons for this unorthodox approach, and claim that it is very successful in picking the right people. In the meantime, it also demonstrates the range of differences which you may need to be ready for in an assessment centre.

Possible Final Round Interview with Senior Management

After all this, some organisations still ask you to see a senior manager before a job offer is made. Don't think that you are home and dry until this important step is completed. Remember also that this is a two-way process – can you see yourself working with that type of senior manager in future?

Exhibit 4.4

Top tips for a successful application

We asked some employers for their top tips for a successful employer. Here are some of their answers.

1. Always read each question and answer it. If you don't answer questions, your application is unlikely to progress.
2. Balance the technical details in your application with how you show that your values align with the employer's values.
3. Once you have completed your application, get someone to check it carefully on your behalf.
4. If there is an opportunity to have an informal discussion with the recruiter in advance, take it.
5. Make a connecting phone call.
6. Get interview practice before you attend the employment interview.
7. Show your enthusiasm: make the employer feel that they are your number one choice.
8. If you are called to interview, make sure you arrive in good time and plan the journey. Even better, visit the area and the site in advance to get an impression of what it may be like working there.
9. From the moment you arrive on site until the moment you leave, people will be making judgments about you.

Jane Hadfield, Head of Learning & Development, Learning & Development, Human Resource & Development Directorate, North Bristol NHS Trust

Be bespoke for the role for which you are applying. Really focus your application on that role, rather than a generalised application. This usually means you need to tailor your CV for particular job roles. Really make your CV stand out – adapt it to what that employer is looking for.

Apply the 'so what?' factor. With a CV or application, you probably have about 20 seconds of the reader's attention, so make your application relevant to the job and relevant to your strengths – otherwise don't waste your time!

Avoid over-long and complicated covering letters.

Be realistic about what you really want. Avoid being general and vague. Stick to your passions and learn to use your time wisely.

Get experience. If, at the moment, you genuinely don't have what they are looking for, put yourself out into the market to get work experience – either in voluntary work or internships – to get the experience to use in interviews.

Ask really good – brilliant – questions at interview.

Befriend relevant agencies and consultants to build a good relationship with them and to make sure they know you and are fighting your corner.

Prepare yourself thoroughly for the interview – know the organisation

Allie Whelan, Director, LeapUK

Understand the values of the organisation and really make sure that you are aligned with them. If not, it will quickly become apparent during the interview, or worse still, when you have started work.

Develop great relationship skills, not just about emotional intelligence but also ensuring that you know yourself and can relate well to others.

Develop a continuous learning attitude and learn from relational inter-action by keeping an insight journal.

Learn to be critically reflexive; this is not about being critical of others, but understanding how much we as individuals create or complicate situations.

Be self-aware, which is not about being humble or self-effacing, but about being appropriately self-aware and self-regulating: in this way, you contribute more effectively within the team.

Patrick Goh, Head of Global HR People & Organisation Development, Tearfund

Learning from Failure

If you have got past the written application stage of the selection process, but then after an failed interview, find out why. It is not enough to hear that there were 'many other candidates whose skills and abilities more closely matched the role requirements'. Neither is it enough to know, as we have seen earlier in this chapter, that assessment methods may not always chose the best candidate.

You need to find out where the specific gaps were in your application and make sure those gaps are closed the next time you apply. So phone the people who interviewed you, say you want feedback and agree with the assessors a time when you can call back for more detailed feedback. Not all potential employers will help you in this way, but the better ones will. This is too important to leave. You have invested time and emotional commitment in your application – make the most of it by identifying where you may need to do things differently next time round.

If You Get Stuck

Getting stuck – scores, or more applications, without getting anywhere – is a very dispiriting experience, and draws heavily on reserves of resilience and self-efficacy and self-belief (see Chapter 7).

Try to avoid longer periods without work. Apart from not wishing to be unemployed, there is some evidence that the longer we are unemployed, the more difficult it becomes to find new employment. Unemployment can become a self-fulfilling prophecy if we allow ourselves to lose heart in the search.

But it is not simply our own motivations which can lengthen periods without work. Kroft et al. (2012) submitted 12,000 fictitious CVs for 3,000 jobs in America, each with similar backgrounds but different lengths of unemployment of up to 36 months. The longer a person had been without work, the lower the chances of being called for interview, despite the similarities of experience and qualifications with other candidates. There may be several reasons for this. Employers may feel that job skills of longer-term unemployed candidates were getting rusty, although the likelihood of being called for interview was actually higher where unemployment was higher in a particular region or city. But one other explanation was that human decisions on shortlisting (as conscious or unconscious bias) and even software to sift through applications may discriminate against candidates with increasing periods of unemployment. Kroft et al. therefore suggest, as we do, that taking work to get on your CV is better than waiting for the perfect job to come along. You are more likely to get work when you are in work.

> You have to keep trying and stay positive. It took me 9 months of interviewing for different roles and getting several rejections before finding my current job. **Employability Panel law graduate, now a full-time qualified Solicitor**

PRACTICAL APPLICATION

For the wide range of graduate opportunities and disciplines that are available, there cannot be a 'one size fits all' approach to getting unstuck. However, the overall principles should apply and encourage you to look at new ways to find a way forward.

The first thing is to realise that you are not the only one, even though it feels that way.

Do not try to deal with this alone. This is particularly a time to:

- work with your careers adviser or with a mentor, someone outside your family and friends who can give you support, objective advice and think about different ways to approach your job search. In addition, having a third party to work with helps to give a renewed sense of purpose.

- network. This is an important time to make renewed use of your networks, and to make new networks as well. This may be face to face or via social media (see Chapter 3).

- make full use of your university careers service. As we have already seen in Chapter 2, our Employability Panel did not always have positive experiences of careers services, and careers services themselves felt that graduates did not make effective use of their service. Do remember that their services will often be available for a period after you leave university, and their help can include workshops and so goes beyond just having a look at CVs.

- think about getting work through employment agencies. This will often only be temporary and may not be that well paid, but it can help develop the skills and competences you need for a permanent role. Agencies need you to be working to earn their own fees, so the better agencies will give you direct and relevant feedback on your application.

- volunteer. Doing something – anything – is almost always better than doing nothing, provided that you keep sufficient time available for the commitment needed to submit high-quality applications. One graduate we spoke to found a trainee role at Harvey Nichols based on experience of several weeks work in a charity shop, learning to display merchandise to maximum effect. Another found a job as an automotive engineer after an unpaid internship with Jaguar Land Rover. Volunteering and internships also give you additional material to include in your competence examples and demonstrate to potential employers that you are actively working.

- look critically at your applications. At what stage do they break down (initial application, shortlisting, interview or assessment centre)? Use this chapter to ensure that your applications are positioned as strongly as possible.

- consider whether you are being flexible enough. Are you too demanding on the type of job, location, salary and so on? Getting started is more important than getting the perfect role at the first attempt.

- look after yourself, physically (taking exercise as well) and in your personal appearance.

- remember that you don't need multiple job applications to be successful. You just need one. Sometimes that in itself will seem challenging, but out there, there is someone who could just do with somebody like you.

- remember that it won't last forever (though it may feel like that at times). In the end, based on all our experience and the Employability Panel experience, you *will* find that role and get your career started.

Onboarding and Induction

This section has been contributed by Dr Jenny Chen.

'A good start is half way to success.'

Chinese Proverb

This proverb is particularly true for those of you who have just joined a new organisation and wish to achieve long-term success and satisfaction in your career. In this section we look at the research and practical advice to help you make a great start.

What Is Onboarding?

'Onboarding' is a set of processes through which newcomers learn knowledge, information, skills, behaviours, organisational norms and values required to function effectively as a member of an organisation. It is also used to describe the onging process of orienting, socialising and engaging newcomers to ensure that they are able to make a positive start with the organisation. Onboarding programmes may include a series of both formal and informal activities, aiming to speed up the process of adjustment and increase newcomers' productivity.

Based on attempts of earlier socialisation theorists, Feldman (1976) developed a stage model to demonstrate what newcomers are likely to experience after entering an organisation. Building on Feldman's stage model, Louis (1980) suggested that newcomer adjustment was not only a process of 'adding new roles to their portfolio of life roles', but also involved a process of leaving a former role. Differing from Feldman's overwhelming emphasis on activities newcomers may engage in after entering an organisation, Louis focused on the newcomers' experience in coping with surprises and making sense of the new settings. Specifically, Louis identified 'change', 'contrast' and 'surprise' as key features of the newcomers' experience after organisational entry. He pointed out that individuals could not erase all the memories of former roles before settling into the new role. Therefore newcomers were inclined to subconsciously undertake role change by interrelating with new settings and using previous experiences to manage surprise.

Feldman (1981) also suggested that role clarity, task mastery and social integration are three typical adjustment outcomes that reflect to what extent you are successfully settling in the new workplace.

Table 4.6 illustrates best practices to help you settle in. Feldman's (1981) Three adjustment outcomes are often regarded as 'proximal'

TABLE 4.6   Best practices to help you settle in

Aims and objectives	Organisational approach
Reducing uncertainty	• Share realistic job previews • Provide a written, in-depth and up-to-date file/guideline on job responsibilities and duties • Set specific goals and clarify expectations • Connect orientation programmes to job roles
Increasing productivity	• Provide on-the-job training and/or work shadowing opportunities • Provide job-specific training • Give continuous and developmental feedback • Provide tools, facilities and resources • Train line managers on how to support new employees • Assign mentors and/or buddies • Organise social events (e.g. welcome party, group lunch) to enable new employees to meet others • Help newcomers to nurture their networks and socialise with others • Implement formal orientation programmes

Source: Adapted from Bauer, 2011

socialisation outcomes in organisational socialisation studies, and proximal in the sense of occurring in the shorter term. Closely related to these are attitudinal variables (job satisfaction and organisational commitment) and behavioural variables (performance and turnover) as indicators of longer-term adjustment outcomes (see Table 4.7).

TABLE 4.7   Successful vs unsuccessful adjustment

Successful adjustment	Unsuccessful adjustment
• Greater knowledge about the organisation and the team	• Role ambiguity, unstable progress
• Increased self-confidence	• Lack of confidence
• Increase productivity	• Anxious and stressful
• Trusting work relationship	• Lack of trust, unmet expectations
• Accepted by the team members	• Feeling lonely and isolated
• Increased job satisfaction and commitment	• Unhappy, lack of commitment, and intent to leave the organisation

Source: Adapted from Ashforth et al., 2007

```
┌─────────────────────────────────────────────────────────────────┐
│                    ┌──────────────────────────┐                    │
│                    │   PRACTICAL APPLICATION   │                    │
│                    └──────────────────────────┘                    │
```

PRACTICAL APPLICATION

Whilst most newcomers experience some type of onboarding programmes, the formality, expectation and breadth of the programmes can vary considerably across occupations and industries. For example, doctors and nurses are usually required to attend long periods of formal onboarding programmes before they are allowed to work on their own due to the complexity involved in the work and the serious consequences of getting it wrong. Another example of the formal approach is when technical workers are required to attend formal training programmes to learn how to use specialised equipment before they are allowed to perform by their own. Those formal programmes are expected to 'minimize risk by providing each new recruit with standard training that emphasizes the proper and accepted ways to accomplish things in the organization' (Salisbury, 2006: 22). In contrast, some organisations prefer a less structured and less systematic method where newcomers are left to the work team and learning usually takes place 'on the job'. Under this approach, newcomers are provided with a greater control of their learning process. They learn the norms and principles usually from the interactions with other colleagues and master the skills from assigned tasks.

Some organisations tend to accept newcomers as they are and newcomers are valued for what they bring to the organisation, whilst others deny these personal attributes and ensure that newcomers accept prescribed standards of membership. For example, in police onboarding training, new cadets are informed that they are no longer ordinary citizens and their behaviour needs to be strictly regulated. Table 4.6 highlights some of best organisational approaches used to help newcomers settle down.

What Can You Do to Settle in Successfully?

To reduce uncertainty and stress associated with the onboarding process, you should learn about your organisations, job roles and social relations (see Table 4.8).

In addition to learning, research has found positive relationships between newcomers' information-seeking behaviours and a number of socialisation outcomes, such as job satisfaction, organisational commitment, job performance and negative relationships with work anxiety and intention to turnover (Chen, 2010; Bauer et al., 2007). The implication is that it is vitally important for you to engage in various proactive behaviours during and after the onboarding process. You should actively take part in those behaviours without being asked.

More recently Cooper-Thomas and Burke (2012) revealed a list of proactive behaviours that newcomers may take part in to make sense of the workplace and reduce the levels of uncertainty, which they

TABLE 4.8   Content of learning during onboarding

Learning areas	Examples on what to learn
Understanding of the company	• Organisational strategies, mission statement, values, culture, history, code of ethics, core business and services • Rules and policies: compensation and benefits packages (e.g. forms and procedures), health and safety guidelines • Housekeeping: eating facilities, equipment, parking guidelines • Communication information: key executives, key contact, reporting system, union representatives, help line
Knowledge of the job role	• Performance review: how, when and by whom your performance will be evaluated • Work hours, job location, requirements, key tasks and duties, expectations, priorities, responsibilities and authorities • Promotion opportunities, career paths, professional training, role models, career sources and available support
Information within the team	• Both formal and informal power structure within the team • Unwritten rules of conduct and behaviours developed by the team members • People to contact for learning about job skills • Information on self-position and self-image

Source: Adapted from Jablin, 2001 and Morrison, 1993

classified into three categories: mutual development (e.g. networking, boss relationship building); change self (e.g. performance feedback seeking, monitoring); and change role or environment (e.g. redefine job, change work procedures). Details are presented in Table 4.9.

TABLE 4.9   Your can-do list: examples of proactive behaviour

Dimension	Examples of proactive behaviour
Mutual development	• Developing workplace networks with your colleagues • Exchanging resources with your colleagues • Negotiating job duties and the methods of performing tasks • Building a good work relationship with your boss • Taking part in social activities organised by the group and the organisation
Change self	• Seeking performance-related information from your colleagues and supervisors • Trying to respond to situations in a positive way • Trying to emulate the ways your colleagues behave in order to achieve better outcomes

(Continued)

TABLE 4.9   (Continued)

Dimension	Examples of proactive behaviour
Change role or environment	• Minimising new role requirements to achieve a better fit to your current skills and abilities
	• Redefining the job duties and work methods
	• Testing limits by carrying out work in your preferred way and seeking if it works
	• Gaining credibility in order to have more influence
	• Delegate responsibilities

Source: Adapted from Cooper-Thomas and Burke, 2012

In conclusion, onboarding is a continuous process and you are expected to become a functional organisational member by the end of it. Most organisations are able to provide various practices to help you to settle in. Even so, you should also take the initiative to learn and to integrate into the team and culture as quickly as you can with an eye to your own personal development.

Conclusion

For some, finding their niche in the employment market – employability – is a sprint. But for others it will take longer, and may turn into a marathon. The more preparation you put into it, from school, early years at university and in the application process itself, the more successful you are likely to be. In this chapter we have looked at how to make the most of the opportunities we discussed in Chapter 3.

So far we have undertaken the challenging task of preparing for your career and successfully finding work. Settling into the new organisation is, of course, the start of the next stage. For the remainder of the book, we will look more carefully at the world of work and how you can really develop your hard-won career and make the most of it. We start with what has consumed most of your life so far – learning – but with a new emphasis on learning at work.

ACTION

• Having read this chapter, we suggest that you think about the following action points: If you think you want to run your own business, there are many sites offering advice, and organisations offering more tangible support too. See The Start Up Donut at www.startupdonut.co.uk/startup/

> start-up-business-ideas/running-a-business/eight-reasons-to-start-your-own-business-when-you-graduate and the UK Government website www.gov.uk/starting-up-a-business/start-with-an-idea.
>
> • Look again at the key stages in the process of finding work, and our sections on competences, smarter CVs and preparing for assessment. Have you done as much as you can? Have you prioritised time to do this?

Further Reading

Browse your careers service for ideas.

One good source of information – and thinking about your next steps – is *Postgrad* magazine, published by Prospects (see www.prospects.ac.uk). Updated regularly, this contains articles and advertisements for opportunities after your degree, and includes ideas on postgraduate study. Disciplines covered include arts and humanities, science technology and engineering, business, consulting and management, social sciences, and teaching and education.

5

Workplace Learning and Development

In this chapter we consider the main tools for your personal learning and longer-term development. There are three key reasons for the emphasis on workplace learning:

- First, and most obviously, to align your values with those of your work organisation and to enable you to perform effectively in that first role.
- Second, to enable you to develop professionally, inside or outside the organisation, in the short to medium term.
- Third, for your longer-term career development and your employability – maximising your longer-term potential to align with your dreams and ambitions.

The first of these reasons is the most obvious to manage, and is most likely to be supported by your work organisation. In contrast, the third is the most nebulous – not least because it is very possible that you are preparing yourself for a longer-term role which may not even exist yet. All three need careful attention. The difference between these aims and your earlier learning is that, this time, you have the personal responsibility for what you do.

Exhibit 5.1

Learning and Long-term Employability

For longer-term employability I look for how well people express their ideas and thinking: to see how far they have an appetite for further knowledge – a hunger, and a reason, for further growth; and to understand their future career dreams. Some of this can be judged from what candidates have done earlier in their education, such as travel, Duke of Edinburgh scheme, societies and positions of responsibility. They show how someone is keen to develop.

Allie Whelan, Director, LeapUK

Understanding How We Learn

Before we look at the resources available to help us learn, it is worthwhile to review how we learn – and think about our personal learning styles.

Most commonly used is Honey and Mumford's (1986) learning styles approach. They suggested that we learn in four ways:

Activists: who learn by having an active involvement in concrete tasks and relatively short-term tasks.

Reflectors: who review and reflect, stand back, listen, and think. Reflectors need to take care not to be seen as 'quiet' or day-dreaming.

Theorists: who learn by taking on new situations, but need to relate these to theory. Reflectors need to be aware that absorbing new ideas might distance them from day-to-day situations.

Pragmatists: who learn by linking between new information and real-life problems. Pragmatists like techniques which can be applied immediately.

Individuals can evaluate their current learning styles by undertaking one of the many Honey and Mumford learning styles inventories, which are widely available. Whilst there is no 'right' or 'wrong' learning style mix, it is better to have a good balance of each style. For example, if your learning style is mainly reflector, you may achieve deep insight into what is happening around you, but you may be seen in the workplace as not living in the here and now. In contrast, activists, who certainly do live in the here and now, may find that in their desire to get things done they fail to notice things and repeat previous mistakes.

PRACTICAL APPLICATION

This short review of learning styles reminds us that to be fully effective learners we need a range of styles. In this way we are more likely to take full opportunity of learning and development from our work environments.

Furthermore, it is worthwhile to bear in mind that our preferred styles may also reflect on how we come across in the workplace. In this way, learning styles are not only important for understanding how we develop, but they also give good clues to how we may be perceived in the workplace. For example, reflectors may feel uncomfortable speaking up in team meetings or in giving presentations. It is therefore worthwhile to consider your learning styles: if you have areas of weakness, look for opportunities in the workplace to find new balance with these. Table 5.1 gives some practical ideas on how you could manage this.

Training, Learning and Development

You may hear the terms 'training', 'learning' and 'development' being used interchangeably. In fact they have different points of emphasis, and it is important to recognise those differences:

- **Training** is the process to enhance work performance and improve current or special personal knowledge, skills and attitudes so that a job is performed accurately, effectively and ensures continuing improvement of work quality (Romanowska, 1993). On the other hand, Bramley (2003: 4) defines training as the process 'which is planned to facilitate learning so that people can become more effective in carrying out aspects of their work.'
- **Learning** aims to deliver qualitative and relatively permanent change in how an individual sees, experiences or understands something in the real world (Marton and Ramsden, 1988).
- **Development** is a more wide-ranging, longer-term concept. Nadler and Wiggs (1986) see development as preparation of employees for an uncertain future. It may include linking the organisation's strategy and retention strategy for employees, and linking career with learning plans. In terms of employability, development may also include learning and experience outside the immediate organisational boundaries.

TABLE 5.1   Balancing learning styles

Learning style	Strengths	Possible weakness: why this matters	Practical steps to address
Activist	Seen as getting on with it. Less likely to be resistant to change	The work usually gets done, but at what cost? May do too much yourself (or try to give that impression). May take risks in determination to deliver	You get the work done, but how effective are you? Balance your style with stepping back and thinking about things – use a learning journal or read a few articles or books – lift your head above the parapet!
Theorist	Understands the wider, deeper issues. May be leading edge as new ideas are explored	Too interested in theory and not living in the real world. May be seen as indecisive, or slow to complete work	Look at activist and pragmatist styles. How, particularly, can you make decisions or explain actions in more practical terms?
Reflector	Thoughtful and careful. Sees the deeper meaning. Good at problem solving. Good at data review and listening	Too much a day-dreamer, questions the 'what, why and how' without getting on with work. May be seen as indecisive or slow to complete work	How comfortable are you in group situations? Make and take opportunities to speak up in team meetings or give presentations. If it helps, get a colleague to give feedback in how you did. Build your confidence
Pragmatist	Down to earth, and happy to put new ideas into practice	A focus on technique and practical application may mean that people or policy may be overlooked	Spend more time listening to others, especially on implementation practicalities. Be careful of those shortcuts: they could yet get you into serious trouble

As you look at your learning plan, remember that you will have each of these elements, and access a range of different facilities to develop your learning.

Reflective and Action Learning

Action learning (and its closely linked concept of reflective learning) is an approach to practical learning originally developed by Professor Reg Revans. Revans believed that real learning only took place when it was supported by real-world experiences – not in formal courses and lecture theatres. Despite being a business school professor himself, Revans was damming of the position of those business school professors who had little or no experience of the real world – so much so that, in the end, he resigned from his position at Manchester Business School.

Although recognising that the detail of action learning may vary, Marquardt and Banks (2010) note that the underlying common principles of the approach are:

- **Real work experience:** learning is acquired in the midst of action and dedicated to the task at hand.
- **Based on actual organisational experience and personal development:** participants work on problems aimed at organisational as well as personal development and the intersection between them.
- **Peer learning:** learners work in peer learning teams to support and challenge each other.
- **Learning to learn:** users demonstrate learning-to-learn aptitude entailing a search for fresh questions over expert knowledge (based Marquaradt and Banks, on 2010: 159–160).

There is limited empirical evidence as to why action learning should be as successful but it is claimed that action learning repays the cost of the learning by five to twenty-five times. Even so, as a form of learning, its practicality and closer link with real-life workplace issues means that it remains a popular and widely used concept.

PRACTICAL APPLICATION

Reflective and action learning need your personal investment in time and thinking about workplace successes and failures. In Appendix E we show a model action learning log.

Best Value Learning and Development?

Despite the investments made in designing and delivering learning and development solutions, it does not follow that those which are the most expensive (e.g. attendance on an external course or conference) are the most effective.

CIPD surveys consistently suggest that learning closest to the workplace is the most effective. In-house development programmes (52 per cent), coaching by line managers (46 per cent), on-the-job training (29 per cent), job rotation, job shadowing and secondments (23 per cent) are consistently rated as the most effective (CIPD, 2012). Other forms of training, such as audio and video tapes (2 per cent), e-learning (11 per cent), external conferences and workshops (14 per cent), and formal education and courses (12 per cent) are rated amongst the least effective. Learning methods such as non-managerial coaching, mentoring, action learning sets and internal knowledge-sharing events fall within the mid-range of perceived effectiveness (CIPD, 2012).

PRACTICAL APPLICATION

For long-term employability, including development within your role, developing your workplace learning is important throughout your career. Therefore whether you are in an organisation that organises training for you or in one where little attention is given to your learning, you need to keep an up-to-date learning plan covering what you need to do in the next 12–18 months.

Your learning comes from a number of sources:

- Ensuring that you have the ability to deliver all elements of your role description and performance objectives.
- If, as we recommend, you keep a reflective learning log (see Appendix E for an example), look at gap areas in your performance and work out how to close them.
- Keep examples of your competences up to date (see Table 3.2). Look at areas of competence strength – how can you develop these for the future? Look at areas of weakness in your competences – how will you cover these?
- Express your learning plan in SMART terms (Specific, Measurable [what success looks like], Achievable, Realistict and Timed).
- Look at your longer-term objectives and what you need to develop to be credible in those areas.
- Check your plans with your line manager.
- Discuss your plans with your mentor.

Some organisations (including an aerospace company we spoke to) in the UK use a 70:20:10 ratio to guide a balance of learning, with 70 per cent related to the job and role, 20 per cent from social learning such as mentoring and networking, and 10 per cent related to course attendance. Other organisations, such as the RHP Group, have a nominal monetary budget to support individual learning, which is used in addition to direct work-related training. Mentoring and how professional bodies require undertaking continuing professional development with your professional bodies are also important in developing your learning, and we discuss these now.

Mentoring

We share seeing the understanding of the role of mentor, as defined on the Alta Mentoring Scheme:

> A mentor has relevant knowledge and experience, and works on a short or long term basis with a mentee to give advice, guidance and support to assist the mentee's career, learning and development.[1]

Mentoring offers the following benefits:

- A separate, objective sounding board.
- A source of experienced advice and guidance on a range of work-related issues.
- An adult-to-adult relationship, which may include constructive criticism.
- An independent role model.
- Someone you can turn to when you feel 'stuck'.

Despite the advantages of having a mentor, they are not a panacea. In particular, they will not tell you what to do (you will need to sort that out yourself), neither will they substitute for the role of the line manager. Mentoring can be used in conjunction with other types of learning, including coaching.

Exhibit 5.2

The Value of Mentors – Employers' Views

Mentors can be hugely valuable in a number of ways: giving feedback and advice, expanding your network and acting as a sponsor for you at a more senior level. The right mentor pairing is important in order that you have effective communication between you and a high level of trust and respect. When you are starting out in your career the best approach is to take all the help you are offered and use these relationships to further your network and enhance your experience. **Sarah Harper, Goldman Sachs**

Graduate 'work readiness' and employability is now very much improved. Even so, we use coaches and mentors during their early development. **Jane Hadfield, Head of Learning & Development, Human Resource & Development Directorate, North Bristol NHS Trust**

---

[1]See http://alta-mentoring.com/ – used with permission.

So what are the benefits of having a mentor? They may be summarised as:

- time for personal learning/reflection
- broader organisation awareness
- broader network via the mentor
- builds competence and confidence
- helps to deal with difficult circumstances
- learns from the experiences of others
- maintains a focus on both current work issues and longer-term career progression and personal development
- gaining independent, third-party advice.

We also know that there are benefits for being a mentor as well. Even if you are an undergraduate, or a recent graduate progressing through professional training, you may have a lot to offer people a few years behind you:

- time for personal learning/reflection (as mentors support the development of others, many report that they develop a different perspective of the organisation, or that it helps them to stay in touch with issues outside their immediate organisational levels)
- leadership: sets an example that can be 'passed down the line'
- learning from the perspective of others
- passing on knowledge and experience
- helping others to 'grow'
- contributes to organisational performance
- gives something back
- supports organisational learning.

Mentoring others is usually enjoyable, and demonstrates to potential employers that you have transferable skills.

Although mentoring benefits are usually expressed as being for the mentees, organisations benefit as well. They offer improved access to, and retention of, scarce talent and present new opportunities for employees. It is a cost-effective way to develop people and, pursued appropriately, should lead to an increase in employee loyalty and commitment. The direct benefits of a good mentoring relationship as you develop your employability portfolio are that it will give you:

- honest, candid, and objective feedback
- support and a different perspective.

Once you are in employment your manager may, at times, also give you advice as a mentor. But it is best for you to find a mentor outside your usual line. Your employing organisation may have a formal mentoring scheme. Alternatively, look to see if your professional body has a mentoring scheme, or ask your HR department for recommendations. If you are not employed, look for a mentor, who may be a family member or friend. There are professional-specific mentoring schemes and, increasingly, special schemes for women (see details at the end of this chapter).

Women specialist mentoring schemes recognise the particular needs of women, especially for those who are working in male-dominated organisations where female role models and confidantes may be harder to find and women colleagues form only a low proportion of the overall workforce. Examples include:

The Mentoring Foundation, www.mentoringfoundation.co.uk/, a UK scheme to help more women reach the very top of large organisations.

Alta, http://alta-mentoring.com/, for women in aviation and aerospace.

Women in Film and Television UK, www.wftv.org.uk/mentoring-scheme, for those with at least 5 years' experience.

Women-only schemes are designed to supplement male/female mentoring; mentoring does, of course, remain open and valuable for men as well. Women-only schemes are usually structured and formalised. The schemes are lawful in the UK as part of 'positive action' or 'positive support' diversity programmes. The value of the schemes can be judged by some of the comments that mentees have given on the value of their schemes, For example:

'The mentoring scheme fosters an incredibly supportive and safe environment to openly identify obstacles (both professional and personal), push boundaries, learn new skills, ask questions and take risks.' **Fleur Jago, Producer (Mentee 2014) WFTV Mentoring Scheme, used with permission**

Continuing Professional Development (CPD)

Whether CPD is a voluntary or mandatory part of your professional development, it should keep you up to date with the technical aspects of your work and help you to ensure that your personal skills remain appropriate and relevant. Friedman (2012) surveyed 102 professional bodies and found that 55 had their own definitions of CPD. Our own definition of CPD is:

A methodical approach to maintain and improve professional and personal skills, to enable personal work effectiveness throughout an individual's career.

Looking at the overall effectiveness of CPD, Friedman (2012) found that use of CPD was widespread (indeed, Gold and Smith, 2010, estimated that about 20 per cent of UK employees had their own CPD plans). However, there were some concerns about the use of CPD. For example, some regulatory bodies may see CPD as a form of public protection; however, it may equally be thought of as weak unless it is underpinned by legislation. On the other hand, where organisations wish to reinforce their own distinctive brand or culture, they may prefer to reinforce their own learning styles rather than rely on generic CPD approaches from national professional bodies.

PRACTICAL APPLICATION

We see CPD as an essential part of employability, though we recognise that employers may or may not see it as important in your development. If you are in an organisation which encourages your learning, CPD provides an invaluable framework for your development. If you are in an organisation which pays little attention to your development, your CPD programme will help you to maintain the skills that will enhance your employability where you are, and support you if you leave that employer.

Many professional bodies have their own CPD frameworks. As an example, abstracts from the CPD framework for dentistry are shown in Exhibit 5.3. Review your CPD twice a year and make sure that it is realistic and continues to develop your skills and competences.

Your CPD may include an action plan for:

- Your developing competences – how you work with others, not just your technical skills (Table 3.2).
- Developing technical knowledge and skills.
- Coaching and mentoring (see Table 5.2 at the end of the chapter).
- Ensuring that you use all types of learning styles in your development (see Table 5.1).
- Reflective practice and action learning (see Table 5.1 and the example in Appendix E).
- Conventional learning through formal courses.
- General reading and activities which are 'outside the box' and enable you to take a broader perspective.

Exhibit 5.3

CPD and Professionalism – an Example for Dental Professionals

Some professional bodies have strict CPD requirements, which may also be established in law. In the example below we have shown an abstract from the General Dental Council's (GDC) requirements for CPD. Dental professional are advised to refer to the original source for the full requirements.

Notice the breadth of CPD examples which are given, as well as the importance attached to formal recording of CPD activities and minimum time commitments. Notice also that CPD is a legal requirement.

Keeping skills and knowledge up to date throughout your career is at the heart of what it means to be a dental professional.

We require you to do CPD because the GDC's purpose is to protect patients and the public. CPD helps to maintain public confidence in the dental register by showing that dental professionals are staying up to date. This is so you can give your patients the best possible treatment and make an effective contribution to dentistry in the UK.

The CPD scheme

CPD makes an important contribution to patient safety and is a requirement for continued registration with the GDC.

The GDC's current requirements have been in place since 2008 and they are set out in law. These can be found at the GDC's website at www.gdc-uk. org/governancemanual. You must meet our requirements to maintain your registration or restore to the register. Our requirements are based on a minimum number of hours of CPD that you must do during the five-year CPD cycle that applies to you. We will require you to tell us about all the CPD you have done at the end of your five-year CPD cycle. We will also invite you to provide us with certain information each year about the CPD you have done during your CPD cycle.

Definition of CPD

CPD for dental professionals is defined in law as lectures, seminars, courses, individual study and other activities that can be included in your CPD record if it can be reasonably expected to advance your professional development as a dentist or dental care professional and is relevant to your practice or intended practice.

Examples of types of CPD may include:

- courses and lectures
- training days
- peer review

- clinical audit
- reading journals
- attending conferences
- e-learning activity.

Visit www.gdc-uk.org for some suggestions on how to carry out your CPD.

Source: Abstract taken from 'Continuing Professional Development for Dental Professionals', General Dental Council (2013) and used with permission

Performance Reviews

Assessment doesn't stop at university, and most employers adopt some form of employee performance review (also known as 'performance appraisals'). The aims of the performance review process are objectives, feedback and evaluation (Storey and Sisson, 1993). In turn, this typically involves:

- linking your work objectives to those of the team and the organisation
- monitoring progress against SMART (**S**pecific, **M**easurable, **A**chievable, **R**ealistic and **T**imed) work objectives
- looking at your current and future learning and development needs
- understanding how the work environment may have helped, or obstructed, your performance
- updating your SMART work objectives for the coming review period
- accepting the results of 360-degree feedback (in some organisations) (see following section)
- understanding whether there is any additional support you may need to do your job effectively
- giving feedback to your manager.

In some organisations, especially in the commercial sector, performance reviews are often linked to pay or bonus reviews; a minimum threshold of good performance will be required for you to receive a pay review. Some performance review schemes may end with an 'overall rating' – that you were 'good', 'very good', 'not good enough' and so on. Furthermore, and especially during graduate development periods, your performance reviews and an updated assessment of your competences (see Chapter 3) will often be used as part of your development assessment, and possibly of your standing on talent management programmes (see 'Talent Programmes' below). Where there are internal job selection processes, they may be used as part as selection assessment. In those occasions where organisations either restructure or need to implement redundancy programmes, performance reviews may also be used as an important de-selection criterion, so it is important to get them as right as possible.

So what might go wrong with performance reviews? Important as they are, performance reviews can go wrong. Poor reviews may be:

- infrequent (e.g. only annually)
- a monologue from the manager
- a review only of failures and omissions (or an excessively glossy review which fails to look at setbacks)
- based on impressions, not measurement of work against objectives
- a disagreement between the employee and the manager
- that both parties are left feeling disgruntled and the employee demotivated.

Qualitative performance objectives may be difficult to assess objectively, whereas quantitative goals (budget management, hitting date objectives, sales, project time lines etc.) concentrate too much on the numbers and not enough about the circumstances (good or bad) in which you worked.

The research on performance management systems underlines many of the problems associated with this technique of management. For example, it is not always easy for managers to make objective distinctions in performance (Heneman, 1992; Wiese and Buckley, 1998). In turn, this makes overall ratings more difficult to get right. Managers themselves may feel ill prepared or insufficiently trained to undertake appraisals. Crush (2013) noted that appraisals can go wrong when neither party comes away from the review meeting 'any the wiser', an excessive focus on what needs to be done rather than how it is done, a failure to have clear work objectives, a tendency for employees to feel disengaged and a failure to give praise. Overall, it is little wonder that so much has been expected of performance review as a process, and yet that potential has not yet been fully delivered.

Against the difficulties associated with performance reviews, organisations are often looking both to improve appraiser training and develop clear policy. One area of emerging interest is 'abolishing' the formal annual performance appraisal. In its place, organisations such as Accenture (management consultants), Microsoft, Gap, and Expedia are said to be introducing more frequent, less formalised schemes (Kirton, 2015:10). For many, this would in any case reflect the type of good practice which could already be integrated into current schemes. It will be interesting to see how these schemes develop, and whether they genuinely achieve the aims of a good review suggested by Stone and Heen (2014): appreciation, evaluation, coaching.

360-Degree Feedback

As part of your performance reviews (sometimes used for graduate development, though typically used from junior management roles and above), you may take part in 360-degree feedback.

This feedback on your work performance should remain relevant to the role, but benefit from a broad range of stakeholders. You will be invited to gather feedback from a range of contributors (subordinates, peers, managers and customers) (Chen and Naquin, 2006).

As to how effective and useful 360-degree feedback is, CIPD (2012) found that 22 per cent of organisations rated 360-degree feedback as effective for talent management (against only 3 per cent for assessment centres).

But 360-degree feedback also has its critics. These include lack of clarity on purpose, use only to deal with under-performers (in some cases), potential breach of confidentiality, lack of measurement effectiveness, treating it as an end in itself, not part of a wider process, and poor communication with those involved (Wimer and Nowack, 1998). At a more practical (and potentially cynical) level, the value of the feedback may also depend on who chooses the 360 responders, and whether the review is for genuine, confidential development or is constructed as part of a flattering performance review.

PRACTICAL APPLICATION

Some colleagues may be relaxed at the prospect of their reviews, whilst other may be cynical, tense or non-committed. This is a pity. Well executed, performance reviews are a very important part of working life and can give you realistic and supportive feedback on how you are doing. You must prepare for a performance review and not leave it to your manager to give a monologue report on your process. Indeed, a well-trained manager should let you do most of the talking during the review. You can prepare by:

- keeping your performance review papers safely (though increasingly, reviews are kept online)
- checking your performance against your SMART objectives under regular review – certainly not leaving it until the next review before you look at them again
- knowing how well (not so well) you have done since the last review meeting (give actual data and examples)

(Continued)

(Continued)

- not assuming that, just because performance reviews have not been mentioned, they will not happen (some line managers still find formal performance reviews a chore and do not prepare adequately for them; make sure that *you are* prepared and have considered your learning needs as part of that review)
- keeping notes on what has gone well and not so well, and why (give actual data and examples)
- thinking about your own learning and development needs (remember, you should have your own learning plan)
- agreeing to new objectives for the coming review period without underestimating the potential for other factors to interfere with your ability to deliver – this is not a mandate for playing games in performance reviews, however, a good adage is to be cautious in promising what you think you can do and then seek to exceed expectations in quality and timing of delivery
- arranging your review date with your manager in good time – don't let your manager, or yourself, be rushed into getting results together at short notice.

In conclusion, the performance review is a widely used system, in all sectors and globally. Despite this, it can still be seen as a complication, even a barrier, to what should be constructive and valuable feedback between the employee and the manager. We have included a candid review here so that you may have an objective perspective of the process. It is important for you to have an informed and 'can do' attitude towards your own review, and use this section to minimise some of the pitfalls in the system.

If your organisation has a talent management programme, your potential participation in the programme will be based on how you perform in your role and how your future potential is judged. We will now look at talent programmes in more detail.

Talent Programmes

Organisations use talent development programmes to develop key employees for future managerial or specialist roles. Graduates may initially be put on talent programmes to focus learning and development investment in what is often an expensive resource to recruit, and one which organisations hope will provide at least some of their longer-term specialist and managerial resources. Other organisational talent programmes may be focused on specialist functions, graduates or to develop more senior – and the most senior – executives of the organisation.

CIPD (2015a) found that about 60 per cent of commercial organisations and 40 per cent of public sector organisations used talent development programmes. Of these, 54 per cent include all staff in their talent development programmes, whilst about 35 per cent focus on higher potential employees only; about 17 per cent of graduates were allocated to some form of talent development programme (CIPD 2015a).

Talent management programmes should link organisation strategy with employee performance and potential in order to provide the organisation with its longer-term functional and management needs. This does not happen as frequently or as systematically as you might expect. Charan noted the paradox that organisations focused time and resources to managing finances, but commented on a 'scant approach' (2010: 2) to identifying and developing their leaders.

Blass (2007) emphasised the interdependencies between talent management and performance management and also noted that performance management (linked with a systematic review of future potential) should be a good basis for talent management systems. For Charan et al. (2011) talent can be identified by ranking current performance and future potential; individuals with high performance and high potential will be ready for early promotion, following a path of development aimed at developing self and progressively leading larger teams and groups within the organisation. Those with lesser talent potential may make slower progress, and not to such senior levels, whilst those with low performance and low potential would come under further review, either for development or for leaving the organisation.

Given the profile and money spent on them, do talent programmes work? At the individual level, Blass (2007) found that only 31 per cent of managers had any real confidence that their organisation could identify high-potential talent. At organisational level, Gutridge et al. (2006) found strategic failures to link talent management and business strategies. Blass noted that although the necessary alignment with business strategy was considered critical, 'in practice they are too often developed in isolation' (2007: 3). Research by CIPD (2012) found that only 6 per cent of organisations regarded their talent management activities as 'very effective', 50 per cent 'fairly effective', but 15 per cent as 'fairly ineffective or very ineffective'. As a result, they observed a slight fall in organisations using these programmes: to 54 per cent in 2012 from 61 per cent the previous year. By 2015, the organisation behaviour specialist Adrian Furnham expressed the view that 'telling someone they are talented is disastrous' (2015: 44): in part, this reflects the difficulty in identifying 'talent' in the first place, but also recognises the raised expectations (which may not be achieved) of those identified as talent.

PRACTICAL APPLICATION

If you find yourself in a talent programme, what can you expect from it? We don't want the experience to be 'disastrous', but for you to make the most of the opportunity without losing your head and sense of proportion. Typically, this may include work rotation, promotions, project work, management training schemes, qualifications, mentoring, secondments, transfers and job shadowing (Blass, 2007). Throughout this time you can expect that your performance will be monitored through regular performance management reviews and future potential assessed though competence assessment. The talent pool is usually kept under regular review, with new opportunities for newly identified talent and dropping for those who are not making the required level of progress. Talent development programmes are not a panacea for long-term tenure in an organisation. Indeed some organisations (including accounting and financial services) will terminate employment of graduates who fail to make the required standards during or on completion of the talent programme.

And what should you do if you find that your organisation does not have a talent development programme? Or that it does, and that you are not part of it? Of course, this does not mean that your development is of no value to the organisation (in reality, whilst talent programmes help to focus development spend on those who are most likely to benefit from it, they are also regarded as potentially elitist). Instead, you should develop your own talent programme. This is not as difficult as it may seem, though it will mean that you need to invest time to do so – indeed, it is central to the purpose of this book on employability. Use the chapters in this book to develop your personalised talent development programme. Once you have done this, use it as the basis for working with your mentor (see 'Mentoring' in this chapter) on your personal development.

In conclusion, talent programmes are still widely used, and graduates may often find themselves on an organisation-based programme. Despite the hype which surrounds them, they have weaknesses in design and implementation. Even so, they are an important opportunity to take and make the most use of – so much so that if you are not on one, we do suggest that you prepare your own programme (see Table 5.2 for an example).

Conclusion

Effective learning and development – throughout your career – is key to long-term employability.

The techniques for learning at work may still include development of theoretical knowledge through reading and professional studies, but will now rely more on learning from your work performance, including reflective learning.

Mentoring and CPD have important roles in your continued learning and development, so do get organised to make the most of these resources.

TABLE 5.2 Sample individual learning plan

	What	By when	Support needed
My personal goals	Achieve 'chartered' status in professional exams	3 years from now:	Can my employer provide financial or time resources to support?
	Enhance all work-related competences in preparation for career advancement		
	Gain further experience in [subject] to prepare for new job applications	Review competence examples every 3–4 months. Look out for new roles from 12 month's time	Line manager
	Keep a broad view of wider developments in my area of work through reading and external conference attendance	Next 18 months: Request short-term attachment to [name of] department	
		Read professional journal. Attend 3 professional body events each year.	
		See if local university has relevant public seminars	
Learning to achieve this	Complete professional exams, review chartered criteria	Ensure I complete at least three exam modules each year	Use competences examples to see what gaps I need to close
	List out my competences examples (Table 3.2), and review strengths and areas of development	Every 3–4 months	Discuss with line manager; keep an eye open for secondments
	Get better at [competency] and discuss with line manager how I can improve in this/these areas	By year end	
		In next 18 months	
	Gain experience outside current role with a secondment/ placement	Within 2 months	
	Find a mentor and discuss development plans with mentor. See mentor every 6 weeks	Ask [trusted colleague] to give me feedback on team effectiveness over next month	Check if mentoring scheme available, or via my professional body
	Is there 360-degree feedback available as part of organisation learning schemes? If not, do I have a trusted colleague who could give me feedback on how I come across, especially in team meetings and presentations	See HR information for possible 360-degree feedback	

Performance reviews are also an integral part of your learning and tracking the impacts of your development. It is very important that you prepare yourself thoroughly for your performance reviews – don't simply leave it to your manager.

Some organisations will still give good support for your learning, others less so. You may also find yourself part of an organisation talent programme, or find yourself excluded from it. Whichever of these apply, remember that managing your learning is in the end your own responsibility. Do take time to manage it effectively.

ACTION

Having read this chapter, we suggest that you think about the following action points:

- Commit yourself to your long-term personal development with a personal learning plan.
- As you start work it is worthwhile keeping a journal, especially in the first year. This will help you to move up the learning curve more quickly. Keep notes on what you did, things you achieved, problems you encountered. Topics to include are:
  - who does what
  - your first impressions (and see how they develop over time)
  - a sketch map of who works where (useful as you get bombarded with new names)
  - learning plans which you need to achieve
  - things going well (how will you replicate this in other areas of work?)
  - things going not so well (and how you will fix these).
- Set aside regular time for that personal development.
- Find a mentor – or two.
- If you are on a professional development track, look at professional qualifications and requirements for CPD.
- Think about how *you* could develop your mentoring skills.
- Take the opportunity to look outside the box for learning opportunities, for example: mix your learning styles; visit a library and browse through the books; think about how the full range of arts, science, technology, social changes and culture could impact your work; go to a talk which does not seem relevant to your field – what can you learn from it?
- Read your professional journals; think about writing an article.

Further Reading

Find a copy of Honey and Mumford's learning style questionnaire (Honey, 1986); look at your learning styles and think about what you can do to make fullest use of each of the four learning styles.

6

Progress and Navigation

Now that you have achieved you hard-won job, the next challenge is to progress through organisation life and make the most of your graduate development opportunities. In Chapters 6 and 7 we discuss some of the theory and practical steps in steering this path. We start with a real-word view of the workplace.

What to Expect from the Workplace

Our 'happiness' with work depends on many factors, and may not even be directly linked to salary – though adequate pay certainly helps. Within the UK, average chief executives' pay can be up to 180 times more than the average UK earnings of £25,118 (ONS, 2015a). And yet reporting on research undertaken for the UK Cabinet Office, Mark Easton (2014) noted that the occupation group which

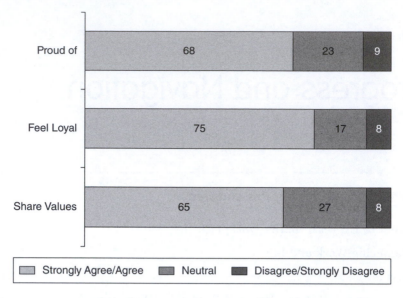

FIGURE 6.1   Committed to our workplace? (van Wanrooy et al., 2013)

was rated happiest in 2014 was religious clergy, on pay less than the UK average weekly earnings, and pushing chief executives into second place in the happiness league. Figure 6.1 illustrates the levels of commitment in the workplace from a study conducted by van Wanrooy et al. (2013).

In addition to thinking about our workplace values, the Workplace Employment Relations Study (WERS) helps us to understand how satisfied we may expect to be at work (van Wanrooy et al., 2013). In Figure 6.2 different factors of employee satisfaction are considered. Just over 40 per cent of us are satisfied with pay, but satisfaction levels of at least 60 per cent are recorded for influence, achievement, the work itself and initiative. The other thing to recognise in this graph is that all indicators of work satisfaction were higher in 2011 than in 2004 – all except job security, which declined in response to the 2008 financial crash and subsequent recessions, which also saw UK unemployment rise to a 20-year high of 8.4 per cent in 2011 (ONS 2015b).

Therefore even looking at work values, work satisfaction and organisation values, our careers are travelled over complex pathways. Your journey will be, at times, exciting, fulfilling, aligned with our interests and values, providing opportunity for professional and personal growth. At other times it may seem dull, dead-ended, clashing with your values or with fragile security of continued employment. Despite the external pressures on our work experiences,

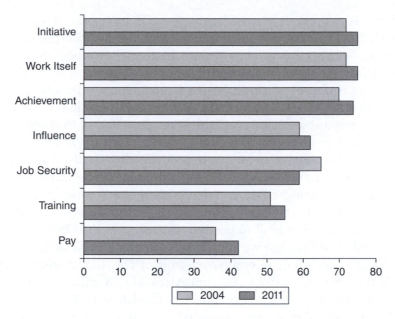

FIGURE 6.2   Employees satisfied and very satisfied (van Wanrooy et al., 2013)

much of how good or bad this experience is can be determined by how well we manage our working lives – our employability.

Balancing Work and Life

'Work–life balance' is a contemporary term for keeping our professional and home lives and our health in balance. It is tempting to think that pace of working life is a contemporary issue. But it is not. Seneca (5BC–AD65 [1997]) put work–life balance a slightly different way when he observed:

> You will hear many people saying, when I am fifty I shall retire into leisure; and when I am sixty, I shall give up public duties ... And what guarantee do you have of longer life? Who will allow your course to proceed as you arrange it? ... How stupid to forget our mortality and put off sensible plans to our fiftieth and sixtieth years aiming at a point of life at which few have arrived! (p 5)

and:

> People are delighted to accept pensions and gratuities for which they hire out their labour or their support or their services. But nobody works out the value of their time: men use it lavishly as if it cost nothing. (p 12)

Whilst it is commonly claimed that the UK has some of the longest working hours in Europe, this is not strictly true. Neither is it true that long working hours equate with higher workplace productivity. UK working hours, as measured by the OECD (2013), show that our UK average annual working hours (1,654 hours) are less than the OECD average (1,765 hours), and leave the UK ranked 21 out of 34 comparison countries. However, the same data shows that most of our Western European neighbours have lower working hours. Working hours may not matter so much if productivity – the work actually completed whilst at work – was higher than our competitors. However, once again UK productivity was low amongst a comparator group of the USA, Canada, and Italy, France, Germany and Japan (the G7) and leaves the UK second to bottom according to the ONS (2015b).

It is little wonder that we should consider how to balance work and life. Within the UK it is estimated that of the 131 million working days lost each year to sickness, approximately 15 million is caused by stress or tension (ONS, 2014). The UK Health and Safety Executive (2015) highlight the significance of continued stress in the UK workplace, based on 2014–2015:

- 440,000 cases of work related stress, depression or anxiety.
- The estimated number and rate have remained broadly flat for more than a decade.
- Stress accounted for 35 per cent of all work-related ill health cases and 43 per cent of all working days lost due to ill health.
- Stress is more prevalent in public service industries, such as education, health and social care, and public administration and defence.

The UK statistics on work-based stress remain high. Therefore, having achieved that hard-won career, the next challenge is to balance your work and life within it. You will wish to be, and appear to be for your organisation, an engaged employee. An 'engaged employee' is defined by Schaufeli et al. (2002) as one who has a positive and fulfilling state of mind, high levels of energy, persistence and resilience; dedication (sense of pride, significance, enthusiasm, inspiration and challenge); and absorption (fully concentrated on work and difficult to detach from work).

But close to the attributes of being an engaged employee is workaholism. This has been defined as the compulsive or uncontrollable need to work incessantly (Oates, 1971: 11), where employees who work excessively use their mental resources to the extent that they feel depleted and burn out (Maslach, 1986).

To be fully engaged and yet to avoid being a workaholic are dangerously close together. Schaufeli et al. (2008) found that a key difference between engaged employees and workaholics is that engaged employees do not feel guilty if they are not working, and enjoy activities and relationships outside work. So, enjoy being engaged – but be careful to avoid burnout through becoming a workaholic.

Exhibit 6.1

Email: Out of Hours Switch Off

In order to reduce workplace stress and the perceived creep of using work-related digital media outside work time, a number of mainland-Europe organisations have introduced bans and restrictions on email use outside normal office working hours.

France has introduced regulations for switching off work mobile phones, restricting email access and preventing employers from pressurising employees to read emails out of normal working hours.

Volkswagen introduced a policy in 2011 that employee emails could only be accessed during working hours, and half an hour before normal starting times and half an hour afterwards

Source: Adapted from BBC, 2014

PRACTICAL APPLICATION

We have seen that long working hours do not necessarily equate with high productivity. What is true for nations is also true for us as individuals. We may work hard, but to be productive we need to work smart.

Our health is important, and so also is our happiness with life overall. Linked with work–life balance, wellbeing at work is linked with happiness, which is increasingly also linked with improved workplace motivation and performance. Happiness, or to express it in academic terms, 'positive psychology', is a relatively recent area of interest in ensuring that employees are motivated, energised, and the business, society and employee benefit from this.

Csikszentmihalyi and Csikszentmihalyi (1988) looked at work–life balance as a matter of 'flow'. The ideal state in life is to avoid under-using or over-using our skills for the difficulties and challenges we face in life. If we under-use our skills, we are likely to be bored; if we are over-stretched encountering the volumes of work and challenges and difficulties of life, we face stress. Instead we should aim for a reasonable balance between the two, which Csikszentmihalyi and Csikszentmihalyi expressed as 'flow' and we can consider as work–life balance.

The key is appropriate balance: continue to challenge ourselves in work and learning, but balance this with time off, exercise and recreation. In turn, this will also make us more effective overall.

Diversity

Issues of workplace inequality are not simply matters of legal compliance, important as this is. Readers of this book will be in a position to improve workplace diversity and equality through their behaviours and long-term leadership in the workplace. Similarly, other readers may find themselves affected by workplace inequality. For these reasons, we have included a section on diversity in the workplace – not simply to look at laws and principles, but to familiarise readers with some of the underlying social psychology as well.

Despite 40 years of employment legislation in the UK designed to promote workplace equality, there are still areas of inequality, whether based on gender, ethnicity, sexuality, religious beliefs, disability or age. For some groups, disadvantage may occur where more than one of these factors occurs in combination (e.g. ethnicity and gender or gender and age). A similar picture but with different degrees of inequality may be found globally. A report by the International Labour Organization (ILO, 2011) reviews international inequality and takes a global view of some of the international challenges, which may include HIV/AIDS, social origin, political opinion and migrant workers.

In the UK, over 75,000 cases were still referred to Employment Tribunals in 2009–2010 in respect of equal pay, sex/gender, race, disability, religion or belief, sexual orientation and age (Employment Tribunals Service, 2010). The same source showed individual compensation awarded as up to £289,000. News media reports also suggest that 'out of court' settlements may be much higher than this figure. In a review of significant challenges still faced to achieve equality and diversity in the UK, the Equality and Human Rights Commission noted in 2010 that there were still gaps in gender, including equality in pay, hate crime, disadvantage for those from ethnic and religious backgrounds and with disabilities, and in the need to reduce homophobic, transphobic, disability-related and religiously motivated bullying in schools and workplaces.

The ILO (2011) points to overall improvement as states introduce legislation to reduce employment inequality; equally, however, the ILO (2011) notes that effectiveness in implementing legislation has been hampered by resource constraints from the global economic crisis, and that in the world of discrimination, as some diversity issues are addressed, new ones present themselves.

Issues in Social Psychology and Workplace Discrimination

Our work performance is not simply affected by how much we know, who we work with, and what we work with. It is also influenced by our confidence (self-belief), which may itself be damaged if we feel we are subjected to negative conscious or unconscious stereotypes.

Stereotype

Most people have stereotypes. They help us make quick sense of new situations – perhaps where someone lives, their accent, their work background, our expectations of drivers of particular cars, the behaviour of colleagues, expectations of particular departments and so on.
'Stereotypes' have been defined as:

> Cognitive structures that store our beliefs, and expectations about the characteristics of members of social groups. (Cuddy and Fishe, 2002: 4)

Stereotype is often not based on objective criteria – it is about how we respond, often subconsciously. Because of this, stereotype assessments and decisions are often wrong, and may also be very toxic because of the impact they have on individuals.

Stereotype Threat

Research (see, e.g. Levy, 1996; Abrams et al., 2006; Steele and Aronson, 1995) has shown that stereotype is not one way – it is not just about how one person feels towards another. Instead, the person who is subject to stereotype thinking, behaviours and work performance will be affected by it, even if that person does not – objectively – believe it to be true.

For example, tests on the thinking skills of older workers compared with younger workers show that (against what we may have expected) there is little overall difference. Younger workers demonstrate 'fluid intelligence' in these tests, whilst older workers tend to compensate lower fluid intelligence with higher 'crystallised intelligence'. Despite the stereotypes of older people being less capable, there is empirical evidence that differences in performance between younger and older people are limited, and may even favour older workers (McCann and Giles 2002). However, when older workers are then told that their test results will be judged in competition with younger workers, the test results of older workers will typically decline (Abrams et al., 2006) . This is the result of stereotype threat: older workers are capable of similar test results, but knowing they are in competition with a younger group pushes their scores down. This is because of damage to their self-belief.

Self-belief

When self-belief – confidence – is undermined, then work performance, learning and aspirations for longer-term development also decline.

Lack of self-belief is also a component of 'impostor syndrome' (Clance and Imes, 1978). Even when people with objective high credentials in education, professional experience and work record may feel they are 'impostors' – about to be found out because despite their success to date they lack the self-belief that they truly deserve it or merit it. (We cover self-belief and self-efficacy again in more detail in Chapter 7).

These aspects of our personal psychology may give new dimensions to understanding workplace behaviour. It is not just about legal and social justice rights, as important as they are. Discriminatory behaviours, conscious and unconscious stereotype, reduce the effectiveness of individual employees and act as a drag on organisational effectiveness.

Contact Theory

How do we overcome the existence of stereotype and its obvious and less obvious impacts on the workplace? Not surprisingly, research in psychology shows that stereotypes reduce when we are more exposed across groups who had experienced stereotype. This is referred to as 'contact theory' (see, e.g. Allport, 1954; Pettigrew, 1998). To illustrate this, contact theory seems to reduce the negative impacts of stereotype – where younger and older workers work together with reasonable balance in numbers and, of course, when women and men work together with reasonable balance of numbers. However, we also know that token numbers (low percentages of under-represented groups) will not in themselves lift individual and organisation performance. Instead, there needs to be a reasonable balance: Kanter (1977) suggested that in the case of gender, at least 35 per cent of the workforce should be female, a proportion which has been reinforced in a number of subsequent research studies.

PRACTICAL APPLICATION

Compliance with the letter and spirit of diversity legislation and policies is obviously important. In addition to this, diversity in organisations is often supported by a 'business case'. Cornelius et al. (2001: 32–50) summarise the business case as:

- taking advantage of diversity within the labour market, so as to reduce problems associated with recruitment difficulties
- maximising employee potential, so as to maximise the capabilities of diverse groups in order to maximise organisational performance, and reduce the negative impact on morale which may be caused by the perceived unfairness of prejudice and discrimination

---

- enhancing the ability to manage across cultures and borders
- creating opportunities and enhancing creativity, with access to new customers and new markets, accessing the knowledge of a culturally diverse workforce.

However, valuing diversity in the workplace is not just about the business case, but also a matter of social justice (Noon, 2007). As well as ensuring high performance with the organisation, the ILO noted:

> Preventing discrimination in practice contributes to the retention of knowledgeable and high-performing staff. This is also important for the reputation of a company or establishment. A policy of non-discrimination sends a clear signal that recruitment decisions are based on the competencies required to do a job. (ILO, 2011: xiv)

In addition, this section on the social psychology of being within under-represented groups shows how damaging stereotype and lacking in self-belief can be to achieving individual potential and organisational success.

International Dimensions of Work

Much of the content of this book has taken a UK/Northern European perspective of employment. Of course, cultures and values differ between nations and continents. A comprehensive view of these differences is outside the scope of this book. However, it will be useful to look at two dimensions of international employment: how values and cultures differ internationally, and some of the practicalities of expatriate work.

International Differences in Values and Cultures

The classic approach to viewing international cultures was originally developed by Hofstede (1984), who saw culture as falling within four separate dimensions:

1. **Power Distance**: Countries which are high in power distance prefer to work in highly structured societies or organisations. In low power distance, people are more likely to question authority and power structures, so they prefer to see power more evenly distributed.
2. **Individualism vs Collectivism**: This explores the tendency for people to prefer to focus on themselves as individuals, or their close family (Individualism), or prefer

121

to organise into groups; in turn, the groups support each other in times of adversity (Collectivism).

3. **Uncertainty Avoidance**: Countries which score highly in uncertainty avoidance suggest a need for rules, laws and strong adherence to codes behaviour and values. Low uncertainty avoidance suggests a higher acceptance of differing thoughts/ideas, and more acceptance of ambiguity.

4. **Masculinity vs Femininity**: Countries which score highly in masculinity have an orientation towards achievement, heroism, assertiveness and material rewards for success. On the other hand, countries scoring highly in femininity are more orientated towards cooperation, modesty, caring and quality of life.

Some typical applications of Hofstede's analysis would see:

Power Distance: Higher for Latin, Asian and African countries, and lower in UK and Germany.

Individualism vs Collectivism: Higher individualism in more developed/industrialised economies; higher collectivism in lesser industrialised countries. Japan is seen as in the middle.

Uncertainty Avoidance: Lower in Latin America, UK, Chinese societies; higher in Japan and German speaking countries.

Masculinity vs Femininity: Lower masculinity in Scandinavia and Netherlands; higher masculinity in Japan, Switzerland, Germany.

Since the original four dimensions, Hofstede has added Long-term Orientation and Indulgence vs Restraint. Hofstede's work has been criticised on a number of grounds. For Osland and Bird (2000) it represents sophisticated stereotyping (and we have already seen the damage of stereotype behaviour earlier in this chapter). The initial research was undertaken in only one organisation (IBM), and some of the populations surveyed were very low in number, therefore questioning the validity of the results. Some researchers have commented that Hofstede's original work may now be outdated, and that in any case culture is changing and adapting all the time. Similarly, we may reflect on how credible it is to make judgments about the characteristics of one country when we already see and experience substantial divergence of cultures within the wide range of organisations within a country.

Despite all these reservations, Hofstede's work is widely recognised and used. We may argue about its validity, but it does give a framework for starting our considerations of differences in national work cultures. The important thing is to use Hofstede as a starting point, and not fall into the stereotype of believing countries and their peoples all conform to the Hofstede model.

PRACTICAL APPLICATION

You may have the opportunity to work abroad at any time in your career, through: international travel; fixed-term assignment(s) in a specific country for a defined period; as a third-country national working abroad for an organisation where your home base is not the same as the organisation's home base; or as an expatriate, in which you spend most of your career overseas.

Be aware that going out on a posting is usually easier than finding a new role (whether inside the organisation or outside it) when it is time to return to your home country. Many expatriates express excitement and thrill (as well as an understandable degree of anxiety) on posting abroad, but find that returning home can seem rather flat and an anti-climax. This culture shock on return home is a counter-intuitive reaction but is well documented in research (see e.g. Knocke, 2015; Bailey and Dragoni, 2013), as is the poor re-integration of former expatriates back into the home base organisation. There is also some evidence (see e.g. Hamori and Koyuncu, 2013) that an overseas assignment does not necessarily help you to get to the most senior roles in an organisation.

But if international work is still for you, here are some points to consider before you accept an overseas posting:

- Be clear about the cost of living abroad, and how your salary will be calculated. You may be put on a 'local market rate' to recognise local pay and living costs – check that you will have enough to live on, and for medical expenses, trips home, children's education and so on. However, if you are on a full expatriate package, your salary and benefits are usually more generous and are calculated to reflect your 'local country' salary, expressed as your home base salary, plus allowances for savings and so on.
- Be sure that you understand the applicable law covering your employment.
- Find out about your home base social security status, 'reciprocal agreements' and state pension benefits (UK employees should see www.gov.uk/national-insurance-if-you-go-abroad).
- Check both your home country tax requirements as well as those in your host country. Make sure that you comply with these as you change countries.
- Think about the challenges of returning to work in your home country at the end of your overseas experience. Uncertainties can be reduced if you have a clear understanding about what you will do when you return to your home country…
- …therefore, if you work overseas but plan to return to your home country in due course, staying in touch and networking in your home country are particularly important and will take time from your home leave to do properly.
- If you yearn for international experience in your role, actually working overseas is not the only route for you. Home-based organisations may work with international partners. For some, occasional international work-based travel may also be available.

Working in Teams

Much of our working lives are spent working within groups – whether they are functional, dysfunctional or sometimes not even obviously teams within the same organisation! In this section, we discuss some of the organisational behaviour issues which will help you to understand what happens within group situations.

Developing early effectiveness to work as part of a team is an important preliminary skill, and one that will carry rewards and frustrations throughout your career. To help you with this, there are some well-established models to help understand the complexities of this process.

The first is to understand what happens when new groups meet and start to settle down working with each other. Tuckman (1965) observed that groups go through four stages as they learn to work together:

1. **Forming**: getting to know each other.
2. **Storming**: disagreements and different views and standpoints emerge as the group starts to work with each other. It is important, as a group member, to maintain balance, patience and relationship during this natural phase of development.
3. **Norming**: recognising and accepting difference in order to work together.
4. **Performing**: settling down to the task at hand.

As you start to work within new groups, recognising these different stages will contribute to your ability to be a successful group member.

The second area of group work to understand is in relation to your role within the group, and how effectively you work as a group member. Belbin (1981) identifies nine different team roles or behaviours that contribute to the success of working within a group. Belbin's work reminds us that a balance of different teamwork skills is required in a well-functioning group. For example, groups without leaders may lack direction, but a group of leaders alone may also fail to progress with the detail. Belbin helps us to understand our contribution within groups and to build on these.

Third, it is worthwhile to be aware of the overall strengths and weaknesses of your group compared with others. Janis (1971) warned of the dangers of group think, in which the group becomes so focused and committed to the task in hand and their effectiveness dealing with it that they lose critical assessment of their strengths and weaknesses compared with other groups. Furthermore, individuals within the group do not want to put views forward that are deviant from the group's thinking.

> ### PRACTICAL APPLICATION
>
> Each of these three perspectives of working within and across groups has been academically critiqued. They are summarised here to make you more familiar with them. During university studies (or work experience) it is well worthwhile to observe these three perspectives and to develop your own styles within them. Group working skills are often tested in graduate and experienced workers' assessment centres. The skills of working within teams then become even more relevant – and stretched – once you start work.

Living with Change

Organisational change is exciting for some, threatening for others. Fugate and Kinicki are amongst many writers who remind us that employees now need to 'negotiate a never-ending series of workplace changes and transitions' (2008: 521), therefore requiring us to be personally adaptable and proactive. For those actually going through change the sentiments may be different, and that whereas the 'before' and 'after' of change may not be threatening, actually going through transition and change is much more challenging, especially if we may be seen as different in our thinking from our colleagues (an issue we have already seen with Janis and group think). Writing in 1999, Edward Schein noted that people do not want to be seen as deviant from the groups they value; he continued, 'No wonder it [culture] is so difficult; no wonder people resist change so much' (p 81). It is little wonder therefore that employees would recognise the analogy of feeling described by Kübler-Ross (1969) in her description of responding to bereavement: from shock to denial, fear, anger and depression, and only after a period which may include a very low emotional state do acceptance and understanding gradually re-emerge.

Change programmes very often rely on clarity of strategy, but even strategic plans can be subject to change. Even where organisations have well-designed and well-executed strategies, it may be difficult to understand what they are doing or why. Recognising that as soon as plans start to be implemented it may be necessary to adjust them to practical realities, von Moltke, a Prussian 19th-century Field Marshall, wrote 'No plan survives contact with the enemy' (1900: 33–40). Perhaps more bluntly, the boxer Mike Tyson is reported to have said 'Everyone has a plan 'til they get punched in the mouth'. Given these uncertainties how, then, should we prepare ourselves for a future-uncertain world?

In living with change, many workers may be inclined to echo the sentiments of NHS workers. In June 2015, Lord Rose published a report, commissioned by the UK Government Secretary of State for the UK National Health Service (NHS), on leadership and change in the NHS, an organisation employing over 1.3 million people. An early NHS Chief Executive (Sir David Nicholson) had described the rate of change as so great that 'you could probably see it from outer space'. One of Lord Rose's observations was that the 'pace of change in the NHS remains unsustainably high' (Rose, 2015: 9). For employees in many organisations a similar sentiment could well be echoed, together with another observation of the NHS from Rose of a desire to see change settle down and that further imposed change would be 'unhelpful' (Rose, 2015: 4).

Change plans (indeed, an organisation's drive to achieve results in key areas) can have unintended consequences. Balogun and Johnson (2005: 1573) show that over 50 years of research on change, it has been shown to be context based, non-linear, and often leading to unpredictable outcomes. There are many reasons why this happens, and Balogun and Johnson explore how the messages which middle managers take from top-down strategies become misunderstood and distorted, even if and when the top-down intentions are clearly expressed. Contemporary examples of unintended consequences of leadership and change, with potentially disastrous results include:

- Volkswagen's use of two-stage engine management software to produce cleaner diesel emissions under test conditions, then less clean emissions under normal road conditions.
- Bonus plans which may lead to informal but unintended and inappropriate sales or reporting techniques, with misselling as a result, such as some UK banks' selling of Payment Protection Insurance which by 2015 had cost £26 billion in bank provisions (Dunkley, 2015).
- Organisations stressing the need for an emphasis in one area of activity, which can then be misinterpreted as de-emphasising critical delivery targets elsewhere. An example has been seen of NHS Clinical Commissioning Groups seeking to manage budgets more carefully, but with the alleged risk that General Medical Practitioners would not make early referral on cancer patients to specialists despite it being known that early specialist intervention is most likely to aid cancer survival, another key NHS goal.

Fatigue with change and the threat that planned change either fails to achieve its full potential or delivers unintended consequences are well documented in research. For example, Kotter (1995) noted that whilst a few change programmes were very successful, most failed to achieve their full potential. Alongside academic research, which demonstrates how difficult successful change implementation can be, commercial research reaches a similar conclusion. These findings come despite the fact that improved change management and project management techniques (such as PRINCE 2 and the Association of Project Management) have become the norm in larger organisations seeking to implement change.

PRACTICAL APPLICATION

Academic perspectives of change help us to understand what is happening during change processes, and may help us to manage and keep a sense of proportion as we live through or directly manage change. Do remember, however, that change often has a high emotional content, and it can be very challenging to balance rational understanding with the uncertainty and stress which change sometimes carries with it. In Exhibit 6.2 we discuss some of the preparations you can make. In practice, every situation is different, and puts a renewed premium on your positivity, learning – and resilience.

Exhibit 6.2

Dealing with change in the workplace

So what can you do in working with change? How, can you help facilitate change in the workplace, as well as to continue to make career progress without being derailed by unexpected effects of change?

Never be caught out, wondering how you can get your CV up to date with the other work pressures of change. *You should, in any case, update your CV and competence examples (see Chapters 3 and 4) every six months.* Remember that your competences will be generic: even if they do not fit within the current structure, they should be of value elsewhere in the organisation. This way if opportunities come up, even at short notice, you will be better prepared to capitalise on them.

Keep your learning fully up to date. Avoid being the person to be deselected because you have not developed all the necessary competences and skills to do your job well.

Ensure that your performance reviews are up to date and, so far as possible, give a positive picture of your contribution.

(Continued)

(Continued)

When the change comes try to avoid being part of the crowd, questioning whether or not it will succeed. (Remember what we have just looked at in the previous section on Janis and group think). Get on with the change and play your part in making it succeed.

As change is communicated it is likely that you will only get part of the picture. This is not particularly because managers want to give employees half the story; instead, they will tend to communicate information as it is known. Change programmes are often incremental. The more detailed picture – especially as it affects you – will take more time to be worked through and then communicated.

Rumours, no matter how well founded, are a distraction. Until you have information formally communicated, try to avoid being part of the rumour mill – either as a communicator or a receiver of rumours.

As the change comes, aim to learn and apply the new ways of working as quickly as possible. Help internal and external customers to understand how to work with the change. Avoid 'work-arounds' – failing to apply the new processes and using an adaptation of the old ways instead.

Conclusion

After the challenge and achievement of finding your role, this chapter has focused on settling in and working successfully.

Research about people in work suggests that most are pretty happy with their work.

Balancing work and life are very important, not only for your general health and wellbeing but also for your capability to perform well. We work best when we are 'in flow'.

Diversity is not just about legal compliance, but it should be the way we work with each other. There are business benefits to diversity, and social justice reasons too.

Hofstede helps us to understand the cultural differences in international work. If you have the opportunity to work abroad, our list of points to consider will help you to start to think about the practicalities.

Understanding the process of working within groups is important, both for graduate selection processes and once you start work.

In your working life you will encounter regular changes, which may include job restructuring. Keeping your employability skills up to date is an important way for you to deal with change.

ACTION

Having read this chapter, we suggest that you think about the following action points:

- Understand where you have stereotypes about other people. Why? What can you do to have a more balanced perspective?
- Have a work–life balance. If you cannot do this for simple reasons of 'balance', build life balance into your schedule and priorities.
- Read and think more about working in teams. What can you do now, and in the longer term, to improve your own team performance and draw out the best from others within the team?

Further Reading

Group work: if you need a better understanding of group-working dynamics and how effectively you work within a group, read the articles by Tuckman (1965), Belbin (1981) and Janis (1971).

International work: for a short review, see Schumpeter (2015).

7

Managing Yourself

So far in this book we have dealt with preparing for and finding work, and learning and development within the workplace. In this chapter, we consider some of the wider and long-term issues of employability which reflect the need for deeper self-awareness, ensuring that work and life are maintained in reasonable balance, dealing with setbacks and understanding workplace equality and diversity.

Organisational Commitment

Where and how we work represents more than the type of work and the location, where work and monetary reward are the only determinants. The concept of organisational commitment is a psychological state which characterises the employee's relationship with the organisation, and has implications for the individual's decision to stay with (or leave) the organisation. Organisational commitment can be considered from three perspectives:

Affective commitment: an emotional feeling towards the organisation.

Continuance (economic) commitment: the personal cost or profit in staying with, or leaving, the organisation.

Normative Commitment: sense of obligation towards the organisation and/or team/colleagues.

(Meyer and Allen, 1997: 67)

Organisational commitment goes beyond a rational or utilitarian engagement for the workplace. A committed employee is described as one who

[s]tays with the organisation through thick and thin, attends work regularly, puts in a full day (and maybe more), protects company assets, shares company goals and so on. (Meyer and Allen, 1997: 3)

For Marsh and Mannari the committed employee

[c]onsiders it morally right to stay in the company, regardless of how much status enhancement or satisfaction the firm gives him/her over the years. (1997: 59)

Meyer and Allen observe that whatever the definitions or perspectives of organisational commitment, the consistent theme is a desire to describe a psychological state which characterises the employee's relationship with the organisation, and has implications for the individual's decision to stay with (or leave) the organisation (1997: 67). Affective commitment is most closely linked with an intention to stay in an organisation and adaptability to change: indeed, research has shown that those with high affective commitment are most likely to cooperate with and champion change efforts within the organisation (Fugate and Kinicki, 2008).

PRACTICAL APPLICATION

We have considered the three different forms of commitment, rather than more conventional motivation theory, to enable you to think about what you really want from your career and working life. As general rule, if you have good affective and normative commitment towards your work, together with an acceptable

(Continued)

131

(Continued)

continuance commitment (i.e. adequate pay and benefits), you should be well motivated and engaged with your workplace. In contrast, low affective and normative commitment, linked with high continuance commitment (high reliance on the pay and benefits from your work), you are likely to be frustrated and feel locked in. Indeed, one research respondent we spoke to, faced with high pay and benefits but unhappy with every other element of her work, described herself as 'locked into a gilded cage'.

Psychological Contract

Employers are required to give their workers written terms and conditions of employment. In the UK this must be done within the first two months of employment and cover factors such as job title, starting date, annual leave, salary and so on (see ACAS, 2015). The contract is written, so it is explicit.

In contrast, the psychological contract between employer and employee is implicit. It is unwritten – and may be unspoken. Even so, it is important in scoping what an employee expects of the employer. The psychological contract is the tacit, mental model that an employee has of expectations of the employer, and what the employee will give in return. But it has no standing in formal employment law terms.

The concept of a psychological work contract was developed in the 1990s when academics and practitioners searched for new and more innovative people-management practices amidst a context of economic restructuring, heightened international competition and changing labour market dynamics. Much of the interest in the concept and development of the psychological contract is attributed to the work of Denise Rousseau in the period 1989–1995 (whose name is not to be confused with Jean-Jacques Rousseau, who developed the concept of the *social* contract in the 18th century).

Rousseau (1995) and Rousseau and Greller (1994) defined the psychological contract in terms of the employees' beliefs of what is expected of them, and what in return they may expect from the employer. It was seen as an exchange agreement between the individual and the organisation.

We can expect the terms of the psychological contract changing as employees get older (Schein, 1999, 1970) because what an individual may seek from a job at age 25 may be completely different from the same employee's expectations at age 50. (We discussed this in more detail in Chapter 2 when we looked at age, lifestyles and generational differences in career outlooks.) Similarly, we can expect the nature of the psychological contract to reflect the social and economic contexts of the twenty-first century. Sparrow (1996) noted that the psychological contract was based on periods of full employment, with employees expecting stability, steady growth, training and progressive rewards in return for loyalty and hard work; in contrast, a more contemporary psychological contract was likely to include competence development, job enrichment, less 'time served' promotion and more opportunistic career development.

Exhibit 7.1

Example of Breach of Psychological Contract in Practice

The psychological breach in this example covers sense of fairness and values, breach of trust, breach of expectation of competency.

> Seeing unfair practices (people getting promotions/bonuses etc. because their face fits); blanket application of policy and procedures; illogical and wasteful actions instead of using discretion and appropriate decision making; line managers that don't stick up for you. **Female graduate aged 24, working in the public sector**

Source: Employability Panel

One of the most serious and basic criticisms of the psychological contract is that it is not a 'contract': there is no explicit offer/acceptance/exchange of consideration. Because it is implicit on both sides, there is ample opportunity for misunderstanding between the organisation and the employee (Guest, 1998, 2004; Boxall and Purcell, 2003; Cullinane and Dundon, 2006). Guest (1998) goes so far as to describe the different interpretations as an 'analytical nightmare'.

PRACTICAL APPLICATION

Where does this leave us in discussing employability? As we look at the values, culture and our expectations of the organisation, it is important to check that what is being offered is what we really want. If necessary, this will mean that before accepting an offer of employment you will need to ask questions and think carefully about the answers, as even in the case of a relatively young graduate (see Exhibit 7.1), breach of psychological contract can be highly demotivating.

Culture

'Culture' infuses how organisations work, and the experience of working in, and with, that organisation. Deal and Kennedy (1982) defined culture in terms of 'the way we do things around here'. At its simplest levels, culture may be described in organisation terms such as 'putting the patient first', 'work hard/play hard', 'you're either with us or against us', 'customer is always right' and so on. Despite the simplicity of these approaches, culture may be easy enough to talk about but it becomes more difficult to define – so much so that Alvesson likened culture to a black hole, so that 'the closer you get to it, the less light is thrown on the topic' (1993: 3).

Edgar Schein (2004) (whom we met in Chapter 2 in the discussion on career anchors) looked at culture at three levels:

1. **Artifacts and behaviours**: the outward, visible elements of the organisation. This may include uniform dress code, buildings, ways of speaking and so on. People outside the organisation would recognise artefacts as part of that organisation's culture.
2. **Espoused values**: the stated values of the organisation. These may be shown in organisation mission and policy statements and may include rules or codes about how to work with each other. Note, however, that 'espoused values' may differ in practice form 'values in use'. When this happens, it may cause dissatisfaction amongst employees and organisation customers and partners.
3. **Assumptions**: these are deeply held shared assumptions which are the essence of the organisation.

Also looking at culture in three tiers, Edward Hall (1977) used the analogy of culture as an iceberg. Hall saw a difference between the

- **External conscious**: the outward signs of culture, such as how we behave, greet each other, dress, and so on.
- **Internal conscious**: what lies beneath the surface (illustrated as beneath the water line of the iceberg), including values, motivation, beliefs, stereotype, prejudice, attitudes to social class, gender and so on.

PRACTICAL APPLICATION

Both Hall and Schein help us to understand that culture is not simply about the outward signs and formal polices which ask us to accept an organisation's culture. By considering internal conscious (Hall) and espoused values and assumptions (Schein), we recognise that culture is a profound concept. Hall reminds us to look well below the water line of the iceberg if we are to understand culture.

In simple terms, all this means is to look well below the surface of the corporate gloss to understand your chosen work organisations. Remember also that this can mean that you may need to confront false positives: despite their proclaimed values, perhaps the organisation you were interested in has such deficiencies in how it works in practice that you would not be happy there, or not fit.

Workplace Ethics and Personal Values

Northouse (2007) refers to ethics as the values and morals an individual or society finds desirable or appropriate.

If you find a situation where there is a possible legal or ethical breach against the organisation, you should speak first to your manager. Some situations may, however, be so serious or so sensitive that you prefer to raise them through a formal 'whistleblowing' policy. In the UK (see UK Government, 2015) you have some protection if you are:

- an employee, such as a police officer, NHS employee, office worker, factory worker
- a trainee, such as a student nurse
- an agency worker
- a member of a Limited Liability Partnership (LLP).

Issues which can be raised under a whistleblowing policy are:

- a criminal offence, for example fraud
- if someone's health and safety is in danger
- risk or actual damage to the environment
- a miscarriage of justice
- if the company is breaking the law, for example doesn't have the right insurance
- if you believe someone is covering up wrongdoing.

The UK policies are clearly set out and are designed to give protection for those who are raising issues of concern. You should, however, be careful *not* to whistleblow to non-connected third parties (the media etc.) as this may constitute breach of trust and breach of confidentiality.

PRACTICAL APPLICATION

If you feel you are being treated unfairly as a whistleblower, leading to dismissal, you may take your complaint to an Employment Tribunal. However, despite the protections which are available to whistleblowers, the practical experience of whistleblowers has not always been positive. For example, in a candid review by the UK Department of Health (DoH 2015) of the implementation of the Francis Report on the Mid Staffordshire NHS Trust (Francis, 2013), it was recognised that NHS staff raising whistleblowing concerns are either not taken seriously or could feel isolated in doing so (2015: 31). The UK Government has declared its determination that the NHS should be the safest and most transparent place to work (DoH, 2015) and have a culture of safety and standards which are as good as those in aviation and the nuclear industry. If you are, or will be, one of the 1.3 million employees working for the NHS, the report is essential reading to inspire you on what to do right, but also to remind you of what can go wrong. Even if you are not part of the NHS, the report is a sober reminder of what can go wrong even in organisations determined to provide high standards of professional care and the challenges of getting things right again.

Organisational Politics

Organisational politics affect all levels of the organisation. It is naïve to pretend that organisational politics do not exist, or to expect that there will be occasions when good logic and goodwill can overcome politics. Organisational politics are often interlinked with cultures, interpersonal relations and group think.

There are many different definitions of organisational politics, but the key themes of these definitions are about the use of power to influence others in order to achieve individual or collective advantage or to avoid negative consequences within the organisation. The main characteristics of organisational politics are the readiness of people to use power in their efforts to influence others and secure personal or collective interests or, alternatively, to avoid negative outcomes within the organisation (see, e.g. Bozeman et al., 1996). Organisational politics often have negative overtones, and often for good reason. It may suggest that cunning, influence and power are used inappropriately to achieve goals. Some of the research certainly bears out this negative perception of organisational politics (see, e.g. Drory and Beaty, 1991; Ferris and King, 1991; Moorhead and Griffin, 1989).

However, academic research suggests that not all politics have negative connotations. Indeed, if a person wants to make progress in their careers, to ignore politics is likely to obstruct longer-term development. For example, to be seen by colleagues as effective and talented (which may include some political attributes) is seen as a skill in achieving more senior roles (Gandz and Murray, 1980). Furthermore, some writers suggest that political behaviour can be used constructively in the application of organisational procedures (Dipboye, 1995) or to use influence within the workplace and achieve change.

PRACTICAL APPLICATION

What can you do to live with organisational politics? Clearly, political behaviours are a potential minefield of working life – more so when an individual assumes a political posture which is based on a misreading of the context. We also know that many colleagues will see a 'political' employee as one who is potentially not to be trusted: even being 'political' in the application of organisation policies may be seen as a potential breach of organisation governance and values, potentially leading to breach of trust and regulations. Drory and Vigoda-Gadot note that positive political behaviours are seen to include persuasion, rational behaviour, assertiveness (not to be confused with aggression), making a good impression and good interpersonal skills (2010: 197).

In this book we have stressed that employability is not just about finding work. Instead, it is about finding the right work, and being successful with it. Employability requires us to be aware of organisational politics. As well as our own behaviours, we need to be aware of the motivations – and sometimes scheming – of other colleagues. This overview has shown that politics can be viewed negatively or positively. In the early stages of career, at least, successful navigation through organisational politics will be more likely if we are aware of politics, but limit our own behaviours to acting rationally, and with respect and appropriate interpersonal skills towards our colleagues.

Personal Values

With the level of competition for graduate roles and the emphasis on qualifications competences and experiences it may appear, at first sight, curious that we should include a section on values. But aligning your values with those of your employer is important, so we will use this section to explain how and why.

Values have been defined as 'a small number of core ideas or cognitions present in every day society about desirable end states' (Rokeach, 1973: 49). Fisher and Lovell extend this definition:

Core ideas about how people should live and the ends they should seek. They are shared by a majority of people within a community or society. They are simply expressed generalities, often no more than single words such as peace and honesty. (2009: 153)

It may seem straightforward enough to understand your personal values and how they align with the organisation's values, but it can be easy to cross your wires, let your values slip or work on double values. El-Sawad et al. (2004) described how 'double think' meant that individuals worked without recognising the contradiction between what the organisation policies required and their own (different) needs and values. Similarly Lowry (2006) found clashes between personal and organisational values which were addressed by 'dual loyalty' (p 174) and 'bracketing' (p 177).

Looking now at organisational requirements, how important are values? It is also a good idea to consider how satisfied we will be with other factors in the workplace – the work itself, job security, further training and so on. An invaluable source for looking at how satisfied we are with these issues is the Work and Employment Relations Survey (WERS). This research is undertaken in the UK every 4–5 years and is based on extensive employee questionnaires (22,000 for the 2011 survey) and 2,680 different workplaces (van Wanrooy et al. (2013). The results suggest that we are generally quite satisfied with where we work. As we saw in Figure 6.1, most of us are proud of, loyal towards and share the values of our employing organisation. Whilst 17–27 per cent of us are less sure about these elements, 8–9 per cent disagree or strongly disagree. The percentage who disagree is relatively small, but with approximately 30 million in work in the UK, this suggests that at least 2.4–2.7 million go to work each day but disagree or strongly disagree with what their employers are doing.

The path to workplace pride, loyalty and commitment also depends on how a profession or an organisation is perceived by the wider public. Sadly, there are few areas of working life or public life which have not had their reputations tainted by scandal. Banks have been fined for misselling and rate fixing, food manufacturers found to be including undisclosed horse meat in dishes, Members of Parliament criticised for misdemeanours such as expenses and 'money for questions', a major retailer under investigation for overstating profits, scandals in the National Health Service, and public bodies failing to safeguard children.

Even the Church has been criticised in a number of different areas: once again for failing to protect children, but also for failing to stand by their own declared standards of integrity, such as failing to pay the UK living wage to its own employees despite lobbying for this as a national wage. Worse still, the Church in Norway found itself under investigation in 2015 for allegedly overstating membership figures in order to benefit from higher payments from the Norwegian Government – a problem not dissimilar to Tesco's alleged overstatement of profits.

PRACTICAL APPLICATION

As we think about our own roles in the workplace, these organisational reputations may influence where we want to work and our own values and behaviours within work. Many will also question our resilience and abilities if we subsequently find our own behaviours and workplaces being criticised.

Exhibit 7.2

The importance of values – employer feedback

In the NHS: North Bristol Trust places a high priority on recruiting people with the right values and ethics for working together and having patient needs at the heart of everything we do. This is not only important for our Trust, but to meet the requirements of the NHS Constitution too, with its emphasis on employee and employer values …. So in recruiting new graduates, we look for work readiness – technical ability, of course, but with the right values for good organisational fit. **Jane Hadfield, Head of Learning & Development, Human Resource & Development Directorate, North Bristol NHS Trust**

In international development aid: … it may not be the most technically competent candidate who gets the job – but the ones who share our values, and who are able to articulate and demonstrate their aptitudes and aspirations. … Understand the values of the organisation and really ensure that you are aligned with them. If not, it will quickly become apparent during interview, or worse still, when you have started work. **Patrick Goh, Head of Global HR People & Organisation Development, Tearfund**

And careers advice, in general, irrespective of which sector you wish to join: Reflect on the type of career you want. What fits with your values, as well as your skills and knowledge? **Dr Tilly Line, Senior Careers Consultant, Employability and Enrichment Team, University of the West of England**

Emotional Intelligence and Resilience

Interest in emotional intelligence reflects the observation that intelligence alone does not predict workplace success. The underlying

assumption of emotional intelligence is that individuals who can recognise their own emotions, those of others and of social situations,
and who can manage their own emotions, will be able achieve advantages in work and life situations (Sala et al., 2005: xxix)

Salovey and Mayer (1997) named and defined emotional intelligence as the ability to:

- perceive, appraise and express emotion accurately
- access and generate feelings when they help thinking skills
- understand emotional-based information
- regulate our own emotions so that they help with intellectual growth and wellbeing.

One of the most widely used interpretations of emotional intelligence
comes from Daniel Goleman. Goleman (1998) identified five 'domains'
of emotional intelligence, the abilities to:

- know your emotions
- manage your own emotions
- motivate yourself
- recognise and understand emotions in others
- manage relationships.

Emotional intelligence has been widely discussed and used, including
in looking at workplace competences, team behaviours and leadership. For example, writers have questioned whether it is intelligence
at all, whether the claimed enhancements of work performance arising from emotional intelligence are genuinely because of emotional
intelligence, and whether the self-rating basis used in a number of
emotional intelligence tests are valid. Despite its popular use, emotional intelligence remains a controversial concept from an academic
point of view, not least because there are so many different definitions
and measurements of its effectiveness (Sala et al., 2005).

PRACTICAL APPLICATION

So how and why is emotional intelligence important when considering employability? First, the concepts of emotional intelligence underlie some of the
materials used in organisations competence frameworks, so it is clearly important that you are aware of them and their potential limitations. Second, and
more practically, whatever the academic debate about emotional intelligence, it
is clear that work performance relies on more than simply ability and resources,
and the ability to work effectively with others is critical. Emotional intelligence
reminds us of the complexity of what is involved in working with others.

Resilience

Resilience is often seen as one of the components of emotional intelligence. In the workplace it is about the ability to adapt and to recover or bounce back when faced with change or adversity.

Having studied hard to achieve the grades to get this far in your education, the path towards sustainable employment is not always easy, though this will depend very much on your chosen career and profession. The high unemployment rates that have been experienced, especially amongst younger age groups, will mean that getting the right job will depend on good preparation for career employment, being in the right place, a degree of luck, and may mean that you are working in a different type of job, at least initially, from your intended career path. But for times when things may not be going your way, resilience will be required. In this section we will look at what is meant by resilience, explore some of the areas which cause frustration in employment, and consider some of the options to take you through the tougher times.

Hamel and Valikangas set a practical test for a resilient organisation as being able to reduce the time from responding to change as 'that can't be true' to 'we must face the world as it is' (2003: 5). At the individual level, management research is less helpful in understanding the nature of resilience. Goleman (1998) discusses resilience as a component of emotional intelligence but fails to provide any clarity about what resilience actually is. Bennis and Thomas (2002) discuss the concept of 'crucibles of leadership', where managers face high challenge within their careers and emerge as more confident and determined as a result of successfully overcoming that challenge.

Luthans (2002) defined resilience as:

> The developable capacity to rebound or bounce back from adversity, conflict, and failure or even positive events, progress and increased responsibility. (p 702)

Youssef and Luthans (2007) distinguish resilience from hope, optimism and other positive attributes. In particular, resilience is seen as the need both to be proactive and to take reactive measures when faced with adversity (p 779). Furthermore, it requires adaptation, flexibility and improvisation in situations characterised by change and uncertainty (p 780). Based on empirical work, Youssef and Luthans find resilience to be linked with organisational commitment, work happiness and job satisfaction, but not work performance (p 793).

Coutu (2002: 48) suggests that resilience can be learned and that the three characteristics of resilience are: a staunch acceptance of reality; a deep belief, often buttressed by strongly held values; and a belief that life is meaningful, with an uncanny ability to improvise.

```
┌─────────────────── PRACTICAL APPLICATION ───────────────────┐

  During the research for this book we looked at some of the things that caused
  the greatest frustrations and difficulties in launching a career after university. As
  may have been expected, the Employability Panel found many causes of frus-
  tration requiring resilience in job search and in early career stages. The results
  are shown in Exhibit 7.3.

└─────────────────────────────────────────────────────────────┘
```

Exhibit 7.3

What graduates report as requiring resilience in early career

Am I doing something worthwhile?

Blackberry (always on duty).

Business is not able to recognise individual's full potential.

Certain individuals can be hard to work with, you have to realise you're not going to enjoy working with everyone.

Companies that don't get back to you after interviews to let you know how you've done.

Dealing with difficult clients.

Difficulty proving myself/seeking opportunities to develop my role.

Distance to travel to work.

Falling behind friends financially and professionally.

Career.

Finding it difficult to identify the right career for me.

Finding it difficult to make the leap to the next grade (pay-band).

Gender bias.

Getting something wrong in my current role that is a silly mistake.

Internal politics of an orchestra.

Lack of a feeling of being challenged.

Lack of experience throughout the business, for example little sales or procure-ment knowledge.

Lack of faith from my mangers in my ability.

Lack of mentor feedback.

Source: Employability Panel N=50

Resilience has been a very necessary attribute for graduates coping with a weak employment market since 2008/2009. Thankfully, the situation is improving at the time of writing. Many of life's changes will require resilience, but we suggest that some of the most common reasons during career are:

- Finding the right role in a competitive market, dealing with rejection – sometimes dealing with no response at all to your application.
- Dealing with early career setbacks, which may include challenges with professional exams, finding that the dream job is not the one for you, failing to 'click' with your new team or line manager or finding that the psychological contract does not meet your expectations in practice.
- Events which have nothing to do with your role or behaviour, for example major restructuring in your chosen organisation.
- Once in role, the job itself may require considerable resilience, such as those examples shown in Exhibit 7.4.

As galling as the need for resilience in dealing with failure is the expectation, as we have seen, that prospective employers look for 'passion' in your next application. Patience and determination are the keys: in finding the right role, you only have to be successful once, even if there are culs-de-sac along the way.

Exhibit 7.4

Resilience and Setback in the Workplace

Example 1: For field staff, we look for resilience to cope with very difficult and complex situations in our operational programmes. In this context, relational skills are paramount. We need people who can work in dangerous situations, often in gated and guarded communities, and it is really important to be able to work and live with each other regardless of age, gender, seniority, ethnicity and other differences. **Patrick Goh, Head of Global HR People & Organisation Development, Tearfund**

Example 2: In preparing the book we also met pilots who had completed their initial military flight training, when it was decided that the whole group would not be required. Devastatingly disappointing at the time, those pilots we met are now successful as first officers in commercial airlines.

Example 3: This example from a classical musician on our Employability Panel demonstrates the highs and lows of carer and employability. Resilience helps to navigate and maintain a sense of balance and proportion.

(Continued)

(Continued)

Lows: As a freelance musician, one has to accept that work will fluctuate, especially early on in one's career. Being rejected outright at audition; not being invited to audition for a certain job; having to cope with the internal politics of an orchestra.

Highs: Winning a trial with one of the major London orchestras; being privileged enough to work regularly with London's major orchestras; doing outreach work for the charity Live Music Now.

Self-belief and Self-efficacy

So far in this book we have already discussed self-belief as an important component of employability and how it can be undermined as part of stereotyped discrimination (whether conscious or unconscious) in the workplace. For practical purposes we use the terms 'self-belief', 'self-efficacy' and 'self-confidence' in this book as interchangeable terms (although in pure academic terms, some would regard them as slightly different). In this section we look at some of the wider research evidence of self-belief on overall work performance and wellbeing.

Bandura (1994) found that a person's realistic self-efficacy to how goals and challenges were approached had an important role in whether or not those goals are achieved. Bandura proposed that there were four key components in self-efficacy:

Mastery experience: having previously successfully completed the same or a similar goal. (On the other hand, failing in a similar goal would undermine mastery experience.)

Social modelling: seeing other people, judged similar to yourself, successfully completing a similar challenge.

Social persuasion: being encouraged by others to believe that you can achieve a challenging task. (In practical terms, this reinforces the benefits of good coaching and mentoring.)

Psychological responses: how you feel (mood, physical reactions, stress levels etc.) at the time you are required to undertake a particular task.

With Bandura's model in mind, a person may have strong self-efficacy if they:

- consider challenges as something to be mastered
- develop (and, in employability terms, are able to demonstrate) deep interest in the challenge to be mastered
- can learn from failures or setbacks in attempting challenges, and try again.

On the other hand, their self-efficacy may be weak or undermined if they:

- don't even attempt to take on challenging tasks
- believe that tasks are beyond their capability
- bring an over-negative focus on things which have not turned out well.

This overview of self-efficacy reinforces some of the concepts that have already been discussed in the book. For example, employers look for *passion* towards the proposed role, and an understanding and appreciation of what a role may involve. Looking again at Bandura's model, this links with mastery experience and social persuasion. As we looked at the negative impacts of stereotype and stereotype threat, we can see how social persuasion, psychological response, and social modelling can be threatened when a member of a minority group feels that they are being unfairly judged in a group or excluded from a group. For some, psychological response may be a major barrier, for instance: irrational fear of giving a presentation, sitting an exam, or a performance, with negative stress and physical reaction damaging that person's true ability to perform that task.

We have already discussed the benefits of mentoring (Chapter 5). This section on self-efficacy also reinforces some of the benefits that mentoring can provide to the mentee, especially in social persuasion and psychological responses to work challenges.

Subsequent to Bandura's work, researchers have found that positive self-efficacy is linked with other elements that are core to successful employability. For example, Alessandri et al. (2015: 783) found that positive (but not extreme) levels of self-efficacy were very important both to job performance and to work engagement. Alessandri et al. (2015: 784) also endorse the view that employees should set realistic personal goals and that training, professional development and mentoring are important methods for developing self-efficacy.

PRACTICAL APPLICATION

What, then, are the practical implications of focusing on self-efficacy? If we are to perform well in our roles and be positively engaged in our work we must have self-efficacy: the belief and confidence that we can perform the role and each of the elements within it. Furthermore, we are encouraged to work to our own individual learning plans so that we can continue to develop our 'mastery experience'.

(Continued)

(Continued)

This learning plan should include both organisation-related training as well as professional skills. We have also seen that mentoring is important to develop mastery experience, social modelling (with the mentor as a role model), social persuasion (an independent, positive, supporting voice) and psychological responses (by giving guidance on how to focus on success, deal with stress etc.). Don't forget also that whilst we may be proficient in most aspects of our roles, many people find that there are some aspects of their role which they find challenging.

Exhibit 7.5

Self-belief in Action

'Doing things and jobs I didn't think I could.' **Communication Support Worker (CSW), age 23, Employability Panel**

'I will never set myself boundaries again.' **Nadia Hussain on winning BBC's Bake Off competition 2015**

Nadia is British, of Bangladeshi origin. Bangladeshi and Pakistani men and women have only a 1 in 4 chance of working compared with nearly 3 in 4 White British women. **Equality and Human Rights Commission, 2010**

Conclusion

Organisational Commitment theory reminds us that there is more to work than money alone. A balance of affective commitment, normative commitment will tend to drive our desire to stay with an organisation (or leave it). Money is also important (continuance commitment), but high reward with poor affective and normative commitment can leave us feeling like a bird in a gilded cage.

Think carefully about the psychological contract you have with your work organisation and ensure that your aspirations are realistic – and don't forget that you are entitled (in the UK) to a written statement of terms and conditions of employment as well.

Culture, workplace ethics and personal values are often overlooked or taken for granted in looking for work. We have seen how importantly employers rate these in previous chapters, but this chapter has reminded us about some of the theoretical models and contradictions, in culture and values.

Organisational politics are often viewed negatively, but have positive elements as well. In your early period of work, be aware of politics but be cautious about getting involved.

Emotional intelligence may or may not have clear empirical evidence to support its application, but provides a useful framework for us to think about our emotional response to work issues and how we relate to others.

Our self-belief (and self-efficacy) are an important part of our longer-term employability (see also our model in Chapter 1). It may pay to have a mentor to help underpin your self-belief.

ACTION

Having read this chapter, we suggest that you think about the following action points:

- What are your personal values? How important will these be when you start your career role?
- Ensure that you have a personal learning plan (see Chapter 5).
- A further reminder to find a mentor! Mentoring has been discussed in Chapter 5. The value of using a mentor to develop self-efficacy is reinforced with the research-based evidence in this chapter.

Further Reading

Think about how standards could become threatened or derailed within your own field of work. Read Department of Health (2015) 'Culture Change in the NHS: applying the lessons of the Francis Inquiries', available at www.gov.uk/government/uploads/system/uploads/attachment_data/file/403010/culture-change-nhs.pdf. Even if you don't work for the NHS, what would a similar report say if you worked in any of the many organisations which have become tainted with damaged reputations in the past five years (e.g. finance, politics, church, food processing, automotive engineering, child protection, retailing, international football etc.)?

8

Conclusion and Finding Your Own Story

In this book, we have sought to explain the excitement, achievement, disappointments and sense of discovery in employability. We have used a combination of theory and best practice to illustrate the challenges and opportunities of a lifetime career.

We have concentrated on how to improve our individual employability: in other words, the book has looked at the 'supply side' of employability. Of course, employability also depends on the demand side, which is an organisation's need for our skills and contribution. We do not under-estimate the importance of the demand for employability, but we have written the book so that, as far as possible, you can remain agile to the changing requirements of the labour market.

Our aim has been to provide a source that can be used at any time in the career journey, especially for those in the early years of their higher education, to being fully established in their careers. Most of all, we hope that you will see that employability – at the time of graduation or later in your career – is not a few ideas strung together. It is more appropriate to see it as a complex web of ideas and concepts. Much more than simply getting a job, employability is about growth, fulfilment and doing the right thing. As organisations inevitably change, the long-term challenge with employability is to adjust yourself so that you can continue to find growth and fulfilment.

Many readers of this book will have over 45 years' working experience ahead of them. Here we suggest our top tips for moving from education to work and then making the most of your working lives.

These practical tips are important if you are to make the most of your own talents. Organisations will vary greatly in the degree to which they support learning and development; in the end, the person who has most to win – or lose – in the process is *you*. So it is important to ensure that you manage your learning and development, preferably in conjunction with your employer, but taking personal responsibility if this is not possible.

Our Top 20 Tips

1. **Start your preparations for work early**

   You need to start employability early (Chapter 1). Certainly, you should be developing a work pattern by the first year of university, but Year 10 at school is not too early to start. Look for placement, internship, voluntary and work experience opportunities (Chapter 3).

2. **Manage your own career – be part of a talent management programme**

   We have looked in Chapter 2 at definitions of career and how perspectives of career moderate with age or generation.

   In Chapter 5 we looked at talent development programmes and other actions that organisations may take to help manage your career.

   If you become part of an organisational talent development programme, great – and make the most of it. If your employer does not have a programme, or you are not part of it, then create your own programme. Keep your learning plan up to date (Chapter 5), find short-term assignments and work rotation opportunities, volunteer, use open learning resources, reading and social media to understand how what is happening may be affecting your work. Find and use a mentor. Within work, look for opportunities – offer to follow up action points from team meetings, take turns (where possible) in chairing meetings, and look for opportunities to 'job shadow' from time to time.

3. **Recognise that you will probably have more than one 'career' during your working life**

   Chapter 2 looked at changing patterns and approaches to career. Twenty-first century career patterns are often fragmented. It is probable that, unlike the conventional twentieth-century view of careers, many of us will work in more than one organisation. Some will do a variety types of career roles as well. Employability is not just about graduation, it is a life-long journey.

4. **Qualifications are important; how you work with others is usually more important**

   Of course your qualifications and grades are important. But as important – in fact for all the employers we interviewed, more important – were the ability to demonstrate soft skills (e.g. ability to work in teams, customer orientation, delivering results, leadership, problem solving, and self-management) and your passion for the type of work the organisation undertakes. Developing these soft skills and understanding of what your chosen organisation(s) are looking for takes time. Eventually you will be looked at less for your qualifications and more for how well you work – and how well you work with others.

5. **Even after your degree – or after further study and years of work experience – you may need to undertake short-term contracts or lower-level work**

   We interviewed 50 graduates in preparing this book. Many had had shaky, even false starts to their careers; with some, we certainly would not have recommended the paths that eventually took them to success. But all eventually found their way into career paths that they found fulfilling. If you need to change course, use the tips in this book to show how your competences (see Chapter 3 and Exhibit 5.1) are transferable. Take and learn from the experience that you do have.

6. **Keep all your employment resources up to date**

In Chapters 3 and 4, we looked at the essential documents needed to be ready to apply for a role: not just your CV, but your competence examples (Exhibit 5.1) and your learning plan (Table 5.2) as well. Both these documents should be updated every 4–5 months for you to be ready to take opportunities which may present themselves, manage your way through change (Chapter 6 and Exhibit 6.2) or deal with unexpected bad news.

7. **Embrace learning throughout your working life**

In this study guide we have devoted Chapter 5 to workplace learning. This is the best route to keeping your career refreshed, nimble and adaptive to change.

Don't kid yourself that you are too busy at work for fresh learning, or that it will be taken care of for you.

As part of your learning, don't overlook the importance of on-the-job training. Take opportunities as they arise for experience in other parts of the business on job rotation, project work or secondments.

8. **When you are doing what matters to you, be proud of it**

In preparing this book we met a wide range of people in engineering, toy design, marketing, voluntary roles, medicine, retail design, engineering, church spiritual leadership roles, human resource management, self-employment, law, investment banking, marine engineering, civil engineering, academic careers and so on.

Important as it was to see people happily settling into these conventional career settings, we were equally inspired by those who had taken a different route to pursue their passions: classical musicians who had a portfolio of orchestral appointments and another undertaking a museum attendant role whilst training in horticulture. Perhaps the most inspiring of all was an interviewee working as a street cleaner (with a genuine commitment to provide a clean environment) who was using the money earned to work on a voluntary basis in conservation.

9. **Get a mentor**

Perhaps have more than one mentor. Be clear and honest about your plans with your mentor(s). They will give you useful objective feedback, understand wider opportunities, gain insight into wider organisation business and politics, be someone to whom you may find it useful to be accountable to for learning plans, and help deal with short-term problems and challenges. Chapter 5 has more information on mentoring.

10. **Make and take opportunities to network**

Chapter 4 looked at various ways we can understand the wider job market and how opportunities may come and go. Networking is an important skill to develop and improve your understanding of the job market. Depending on where you are in your job search, it may be worthwhile to get some quality business cards printed.

Use face-to-face opportunities as well as social media. But as you do network, don't be a network bore and spend time telling others about yourself – ask them about what they are doing: this is more flattering and more effective in developing genuine and useful contacts.

From time to time, go to networking events that are 'different' for you and outside the box. Meet new people outside your normal circles: how does their experience reflect, or differ from your own perspectives? What can you learn from this?

And, of course, send a LinkedIn invitation to those you meet (see Chapter 3 for tips on how to use LinkedIn to support job seeking).

11. **Understand stereotypes; don't be derailed by them**

Respecting diversity in the workplace is a legal requirement in most countries and usually part of organisational policies and values as well. But working effectively with other colleagues is much more than legal and organisational compliance. In Chapter 6 we saw that stereotyping was often the basis for discrimination and that the belief that you may be a victim of stereotype (based on gender, age, sexuality, ethnicity, disability etc.) can be a source of stereotype threat, with reduced self-belief and potentially reduced work performance. It is important not to stereotype others, nor to be derailed by stereotype threat. All this is easy to write, harder to do, but an important basis for working together.

12. **Understand that change is inevitable – be ready to adapt**

A theme throughout this book has been that future change is inevitable, and it is difficult to predict how this change will impact us. Change is designed to develop organisation performance. It is not designed to offend us, even though that is how it may feel at times. Use these 20 tips to be ready for change, and be an 'early adopter' as new change programmes are introduced.

If you find yourself on change project groups, take the opportunity to read round the subject beforehand. Be the 'go-to' person, based on your efforts to prepare yourself thoroughly for new situations and change implementation.

And if all fails and your job is changed – even abolished – these tips will continue to reinforce your own employability.

13. **Understand your psychological contract**

In Chapter 7 we looked at the psychological contract – the unwritten, and often unspoken part of your working relationship with your work organisation. What is your psychological contract? How important is it for you to align your values and needs with those of your employer?

14. **Manage work–life balances**

Easier to write about than to live by, but manage your work–life balance. Be engaged, but avoid developing into a workaholic (Chapter 6).

15. **Keep an eye on changing horizons**

Understand your organisation's goals, but keep an eye on the wider environment too. Read relevant media and use, sensibly and carefully, social media.

From time to time, look at your own and comparable organisation job sites: what impression do they convey; what types of roles do they have that could interest you; what skills, competences and experience are required; what changes are coming and how will you adapt?

16. **Understand your personal values**

In Chapter 7 we explored personal values and found that it was quite possible to have personal values and separate – sometimes totally contradictory – work values. If you find that your values clash, it is time to take stock. It might be time to look for work elsewhere.

17. **It may not always be good – play the long game (emotional intelligence)**

Chapter 7 was a reminder of the need for emotional intelligence (personal self-awareness) and the need for resilience during our careers.

18. **Enjoy it, don't endure it**

Despite the need for resilience and emotional intelligence, if you find that, over a period, you are not enjoying your work – for whatever reason – find a different role. Don't allow yourself to be trapped by thinking that your knowledge and experience will be of no use elsewhere. Follow the advice in this section to keep your employability, now and throughout your career, fresh.

19. **Manage those who work for you without falling into poor practice traps**

As you develop your career experiences you will undoubtedly encounter poor practices (poorly delivered performance reviews, misleading information, failing to address under-performance, failing to compliment good work performance, failure to give a job application decision when promised etc.).

Many of those reading this book will become managers; when you lead others, resolve that you will not fall into the same traps.

20. **Relish your own field of dreams**

Senge (1990) warns us of the dangers of feeling that we are trapped in bureaucracies and losing ourselves in 'fields of dreams'.

Feel the same level of pride and purpose that many of our graduate interviewees have found.

Long-term employability needs us to refresh and realise our dreams.

Never stop learning. Enjoy living your dreams.

Appendix A

Percentage of Graduates Employed by Subject Area 2012/13

Subject area	Employed (%)	Unemployed (%)
Medicine and dentistry	91.0	1.3
Education	89.7	2.3
Subjects allied to medicine	87.8	3.4
Veterinary science	87.7	5.4
Architecture, building and planning	81.3	6.2
Business and administrative studies	78.7	7.7
Mass communications and documentation	77.3	9.8
Engineering and technology	75.8	7.7
Creative arts and design	74.9	8.6
Social studies	74.2	7.5
Computer science	71.9	11.9
Agriculture and related subjects	70.0	6.0
Biological sciences	68.7	6.8
Combined	68.6	4.1
Languages	66.1	7.1
Law	64.7	6.4
Historical and philosophical studies	64.4	7.4
Mathematical sciences	64.3	8.2
Physical sciences	63.6	8.0

Source: Higher Education Statistics Agency, 2014a (Used with permission)

Appendix B

Sample CV, with Annotated Comments

This CV is genuine and was submitted with a covering letter (see Appendix C) as part of an application for a summer internship. The candidate was successful. We have retained the key details of the CV, but changed the names and locations to retain confidentiality.

What Makes This a Good CV?

- Short and to the point (two sides).
- Sets out both paid and voluntary employment and shows how the skills learned were relevant for further organisational life.
- Summarises key skills and shows how these were relevant to further organisational learning.
- We have a sense that we know the person – at least on paper!

How Could the CV Be Improved?

- This CV did not include a personal statement. Normally we would like to see this, but it is implied in the covering letter (Appendix C) which clearly sets out the candidate's aspirations and links those clearly to the organisation to which she is applying.
- Later in her career we would see more detail on competences and skills as the candidate's work knowledge is developed.

Amy Patterson
Holiday Address (20 December – 15 January)
Term Address (current)

(Continued)

(Continued)

EDUCATION

2016–Present: Exeter University, BSc Business Management (International Route) Expected 2:1, Second Year

Modules Include: International Management, Managing People, Organisational Behaviour, Accounting and Finance, Managing the Public Services, Marketing and Strategy.

2011–2013: Mansfield Sixth Form College

3 A-levels: History A, Psychology B, Business Studies B.

2006–2011 Mansfield Secondary School

9 GCSEs: English Language A, History A, Business Studies A, Religious Studies A, English Literature A, Mathematics B, Science (double award) BB, Drama B.

WORK EXPERIENCE

2013–Present: Sales Assistant, Next, Mansfield Eastgate (temporary positions during summer and Christmas).

- Help and advise customers.
- Arrange stock to maximize sales.
- Responsible for checking stock levels.

2012–2014: Sales Assistant, John Lewis plc, Mansfield

- Helped to train new staff.
- Responsible for own area of stock and maintaining it to company standards, as well as ensuring sales achievements in this area.
- Dealt with customers one on one and often developed close relationships with them.
- Attended key business meetings and reported back to colleagues.

SKILLS

- Customer Service is definitely a forte of mine. I naturally find it easy to get on with people, and my experience at John Lewis helped to refine this into one of my best skills. I love talking to people and developing relationships with customers, colleagues and individuals I have met through work. I believe this transferable skill is the main reason I want to become involved in Human Resource Management.
- Teamwork and leadership, I believe, is a hugely important attribute to have in the modern business world, and it is something that I have developed through not only experience at work in leading teams but also through volunteering.

- During my A Levels I completed the AQA Baccalaureate which involved 100 hours of community service, and this really sparked off my interest in volunteering as I began helping weekly with a local Beaver Scout group. I have since helped with the group and over my summer holidays in a local Children's Club. This volunteering has really enhanced my team and leadership skills and I feel more than confident in leading teams.
- I am a very analytical person and I believe that problem solving is another key skill of mine. I enjoy immensely digging out problems and finding ways around them or making a process more efficient. I find myself doing it all the time in various work positions I have had as it is a real passion of mine.
- I love to be organised and sorting things out into a logical format excites me. An example of me combining these two skills would be the internship I am currently undertaking with the Alzheimers Society in which I am creating a statistical report and a written report analysing the quality of their services in Exeter and the Vale to be sent to PQASSO.

INTERESTS

- *Volunteering*: As previously mentioned I do a lot of work in my local community in my spare time.
- *Travel*: I went round Europe this summer and found it very interesting to see the different cultures and the cities, I also lived in America for 3 years before my GCSEs during which time I was lucky enough to experience and see a lot of the different states as well as the benefit of being immersed in a different society.
- *Exercise*: Such as yoga, swimming and tennis, I believe that exercise is essential for a balanced lifestyle.

Appendix C
Sample Covering Letter

This is a genuine covering letter, seeking a summer internship in a major UK financial services institution. In this case the enquirer successfully obtained a summer internship, which led directly to a place on the graduate HR programme with the same organisation on graduation. Whilst the letter is genuine, the name, university and employer have been anonymised for reasons of confidentiality.

What makes this a good covering letter?

- It is relatively short, and is to the point.
- The writer's research and interest both in a professional career and passion for the organisation shine through. The writer has made the effort to do an individual letter, not simply send off a generic enquiry.
- The writer then intelligently reinforces how her own background, work experiences and competences could be of benefit to this employer.
- The writer gives a sense of her own objectives from an internship (in this case, these aims could arguably have been more specific).

Amy Patterson, Human Resources
Summer Internship

Miss Amy Patterson
15 Long Drive
Westfield
Yorkshire YR2 9EZ
E-mail: Amy.Patterson@myemail.co.uk

Mr E. H. Jones
Internship Manager
Money Financial Group
PO Box 22x
Birmingham, B21 7EF

27 September 2017

Dear Mr Jones

Internship Opportunities

My name is Amy Patterson, a second-year student at Exeter University studying Business Management (International route) who is committed to a career in Human Resources. I've always had a passion for people and my academic learning at Exeter has facilitated this and I am now dedicated towards this career path.

Money Financial Group has a heritage and a reputation for being committed to its customers and developing relationships with them, something that I think is essential for any company in the financial sector in the current economic climate. I was impressed to learn that 1 in 3 people have a relationship with Money Financial Group as it shows how well trusted they are. I was also more than impressed to learn that in 2010 Money Financial Group gave £76 million to good causes. I believe that giving back to the community is essential for any company. The fact that your employees are encouraged and able to volunteer makes me so motivated to work for this company as volunteering is very important to me and accolades such as the 'Stakeholders with our Community Award' excite me as a possible future challenge. I want to be a part of this organisation because it is fast-moving, customer orientated and is aware of its responsibility toward the community and the environment.

I have an innate business sense, I always think in business terms and find myself constantly analysing and problem solving. I think this is an attribute that is very relevant to Money Financial Group because in the financial sector there is no room for mistakes and customers want to know that they're getting the best care.

In my current job I find myself looking at the way in which my managers deal with employees, from recruitment to reward, and find it fascinating to compare it to old employees and suggest to managers other ways of doing things. I believe good customer service starts with a satisfied workforce as they are the ones promoting your company.

From my CV [Appendix B] you can see that I have done a lot of volunteering, which put me into positions of responsibility, and this has given me excellent leadership skills. I also feel confident in completing and undertaking projects due to my current internship at the Alzheimers Society in which I am project-managing a research task about their services in Exeter and the Vale. This is something I have found challenging and rewarding, but definitely exciting.

(Continued)

(Continued)

This summer internship is an amazing opportunity for me to develop my skills and apply them in a commercial context. I would love to be able to learn more about an industry and job role that I am so passionate about. This internship is a challenge I would love to take on.

Yours Sincerely

Amy Patterson

Appendix D

How I Got Where I Am Today – Summaries of Graduate Work Search Experiences

---

How I got started in MARINE ENGINEERING

Whilst studying, to what extent did you intentionally use other non-education experience to prepare for future employment?

Casual employment? Not relevant to my later career

Work placements/internship? Often helpful – worked during my studies

Travel? Often helpful – worked at sea during my studies

Volunteering? Sometimes useful

Clubs and societies? Sometimes useful

Assessment challenges? Finding work to apply for; Understanding what employers were looking for; Deciding which job to accept

What do you do for continuing professional development? Yes, I need to constantly develop interests and learning

Do you have a mentor? Yes, but I don't find it helpful

Main achievements to date? Gaining employment; Gaining Engineer Officer of the Watch licence; Retraining as a Marine Engineer – very interesting studies

Key Frustrations? Lack of progression in some roles; Poor management; Lack of knowing which career direction to go in

---

How I got started in CLINICAL SCIENCE

Role Now: Clinical Scientist; First degree Physiology and psychology; MSc in Physiology (sponsored by NHS)

Whilst studying, to what extent did you intentionally use other non-education experience to prepare for future employment?

Casual employment? (especially care assistant) Often

Work placements? Quite often

(Continued)

(Continued)

Travel abroad? Sometimes

Volunteering? Sometimes

Clubs and societies? Sometimes

Assessment challenges? Feeling of heading nowhere [before I got the clinical scientist traineeship]; Not hearing back from applications; Dealing with disappointment/rejection; Time taken to complete applications

What do you do for continuing professional development? Training, conferences, self-directed learning

Main achievements to date? Getting the funded MSc; Balancing work, study and life; Learning to deal with difficult situations in a mature manner; Think about doing a PhD later

Key frustrations? Poor management and organisation; Lack of support from more senior staff; Poor feedback and advice

---

How I got started in LAW, AS A SOLICITOR

Whilst studying, to what extent did you intentionally use other non-education experience to prepare for future employment?

Casual employment? Sometimes

Work placements/internship? Often

Travel? Sometimes

Volunteering? Often

Clubs and societies? Quite often

Assessment challenges? Finding work to apply for; Time taken to submit applications; Assessment centres (group exercises); Group exercises (psychometric tests)

What do you do for continuing professional development? Training through internal and external training

Do you have a mentor? Yes

Main achievements to date? Gaining a training contract; Qualifying as a solicitor; Becoming an Associate with my current employer, despite not coming through a 'traditional route', i.e. a red-brick university and with a city law firm for my training

Key frustrations? Maintaining extra-curricular activities; Finding a positive perspective, despite setbacks, for the next interview

---

How I got started in MARKETING

Whilst studying, to what extent did you intentionally use other non-education experience to prepare for future employment?

Casual employment? Often

Work placements/internship? Quite often

Travel? No

Volunteering? Sometimes

Clubs and societies? No

In addition to these, I found the following very important: Good working relationships with key agencies; Networking; Continuing to attend University business evenings with national speakers – helped to stay focused and continued with networking; Short-term contracts, despite low pay, gave very valuable experience prior to successful selection for my current role

Assessment challenges? Experienced a wide range of interviewing styles and assessment centres (including group exercises, psychometric assessments and presentations). The main problem, however, was finding roles for which to apply and having the time to complete good-quality applications

What do you do for continuing professional development? Yes, but new employer is very keen on both general and specific training support

Do you have a mentor? No

Main achievements to date? Achieving dream job against strong competition; Establishing new practices in new employer which have been valued and reflect both MSc training and personal experiences from earlier short-term contracts

Key frustrations? Length of time preparing applications; Not hearing back on applications; Over two-year period with a very fragmented job record, wondering whether career plans would ever work out

How I got started in SOCIAL WORK

Whilst studying, to what extent did you intentionally use other non-education experience to prepare for future employment?

Casual employment? Never

Work placements/internship? Never

Travel? Quite often

Volunteering? Often

Clubs and societies? Sometimes

Assessment challenges? Time taken to complete applications; Understanding what interview questions required; Psychometric assessments

What do you do for continuing professional development? I keep a log of training I've done (although not entirely up to date) and try to sense check it now and again – [from my earlier career] having to apply for my Chartered Institute of Personnel and Development (CIPD) upgrade helped with this!

Main achievements to date? I am undertaking voluntary work in order to get enough experience to be accepted at university to study social work – complete change of career

[Previous employer]:Achieving senior management position

Getting my Chartered status with CIPD in Human Resource Management

Getting my redundancy approved (previous employer)!

(Continued)

163

(Continued)

Key frustrations? Uncertainty about future career direction; It's taken me a while to get focused on what is really important to me, thus far when there have been setbacks I've tended to get upset then carry on regardless

[Previous employer] – Seeing unfair practices (people getting promotions/bonuses etc. because their face fits); Blanket application of policy and procedures dictating illogical and wasteful actions instead of using discretion and appropriate decision making; Line managers that don't stick up for you

---

Appendix E

Example of Reflective Learning/Action Learning Log

Activity	Went right	Went not so well	What I will do next time
I project led new implementation process	Quality complimented, on time, under budget		Pleased with outcome and would like to do more of this
			See if I can do an online project management course
First half year performance review	Pleased with outcome overall		Wasn't well prepared for discussion on future development
			Cross about this as I wanted to get some things sorted out. Next time, make sure I take my learning plan in to meeting
Asked to run our team meeting about team cost management	Felt I led the meeting quite well. Most people spoke up	Overrun of costs	Cost information comes in late. I thought finance would provide this, but it didn't work. Need to keep a closer watch on costs in future
Launch of new policy and procedure for xxxxx	Long time spent on this and we got it out in time	Some dissatisfaction expressed about lack of consultation on content of final product	Ensure to check earlier with stakeholders next time. They said they hadn't enough notice this time round

(Continued)

(Continued)

Activity	Went right	Went not so well	What I will do next time
Had to deal with complaints about misuse of xxxx		Some angry feedback which I thought was not appropriate, but didn't feel I stood my ground very well	Speak to line manager to book on to an assertiveness course
Busy three months and I got quite run down by the end of this period		Got the work done, but long hours and feel tired. Haven't looked after myself	Make sure I take time off as well Line manager has suggested I look at a time management course Set aside one night a week for sport, and at least one night for gym Have been advised to plan my leave so I don't just waste it. Need to do this
Asked to present findings to senior team meeting	Pleased to get it over with. Comments supportive	Not always confident in presenting to a larger group	Look at a presentation skills course. Have done quite a few in my studies but could improve

References

Abrams, D, Eller, A and Bryant, J (2006) An age apart: the effects of inter-generational contact and stereotype threat on performance and inter-group bias, *Psychology and Aging*, 21(4): 691–702.

ACAS (2015) Contracts of employment. Available at www.acas.org.uk/index.aspx?articleid=1577 (accessed 10 February 2016).

Alessandri, G, Borgogni, L, Schaufeli, W, Caprana, V C, and Consiglio, C (2015) From positive orientation to job performance: the role of work engagement and self-efficacy beliefs, *Journal of Happiness Studies*, 16(3): 767–788.

Allport, G W (1954) *The Nature of Prejudice*. Reading, MA: Addison-Wesley.

Alvesson, M (1993) *Cultural Perspectives on Organization*. Cambridge: Cambridge University Press.

Alwin, D F and Krosnick, J A (1991) Aging, cohorts, and the stability of socio-political orientations over the life span, *American Journal of Sociology*, 97(1): 169–195.

Arnold, J (1997) *Managing Careers into the 21st Century*. London: Paul Chapman.

Arnold, J (2004) The congruence problem in John Holland's theory of vocational decisions, *Journal of Occupational and Organizational Psychology*, 77: 95–113.

Arthur, M B and Rousseau, D M (eds) (1996) *The Boundaryless Career: A New Employment Principle for a New Organizational Era*. Oxford: Oxford University Press.

Ashforth, B E, Sluss, D M and Saks, A M (2007) Socialization tactics, pro-active behavior, and newcomer learning: integrating socialization models, *Journal of Vocational Behavior*, 70: 447–462.

Association of Graduate Careers Advisory Services (AGCAS) (2015) Graduate labour market buoyant, report heads of university careers services. Available at www.agcas.org.uk/articles/844-Graduate-labour-market-buoyant-report-heads-of-university-careers-services- (accessed 17 June 2015).

Atkinson, J (1984) Manpower strategies for flexible organisations, *Personnel Management*, 16(8): 28–31.

Atkinson, J (1985) Flexibility: planning for an uncertain future, *Manpower Policy and Practice*, 1: 26–29.

Bailey, C and Dragoni, L (2013) Repatriation after global assignments: current HR practices and suggestions for ensuring successful repatriation, *People and Strategy*, 36(1): 48–57.

Balogun, J and Johnson, G (2005) From intended strategies to unintended outcomes: the impact of change recipient sensemaking, *Organization Studies*, 26(11): 1573–1601.

Bandura, A (1994) Self-efficacy. In Ramachaudran, V S (ed.), E*ncyclopedia of Human Behavior* (pp 71–81). New York: Academic Press.

Baruch, Y (2004) *Managing Careers: Theory and Practice*. Harlow: Prentice Hall.

Bauer,T N (2011) *Onboarding New Employees: Maximizing Success*. SHRM Foundation's Effective Practice Guideline Series. Alexandria, VA: Society for Human Resource Management.

Bauer, T N, Erdogan, B, Bodner, T, Truxillo, D M and Tucker, J S (2007) Newcomer adjustment during organizational socialization: a meta-analytic review of antecedents, outcomes and methods, *Journal of Applied Psychology*, 92: 707–721.

BBC (2014) Could work emails be banned after 6pm? by Tom de Castella. Available at www.bbc.co.uk/news/magazine-26958079 (accessed 19 August 2015).

Belbin, M (1981) *Management Teams*. London: Heinemann.

Bengtson, V L, Elder (Jr), G H and Putney, N M (2005) The lifecourse perspective on ageing: linked lives, timing, and history. In Johnson, M L (ed.), *Age and Ageing*. Cambridge: Cambridge University Press.

Bennis, W G and Thomas, R J (2002) Crucibles of Leadership, *Harvard Business Review*, September, pp 39–45.

Blass, E (2007) *Talent Management Maximising Talent for the Whole Business*. London: Chartered Management Institute and Ashridge Management Consulting.

Boudreau, J W, Jesuthasan, R and Creelman, D (2015) *Lead the Work: Navigating a World Beyond Employment*. San Francisco, CA: Jossey-Bass.

Boxall, P and Purcell, J (2003) *Strategy and Human Resource Management*. Basingstoke: Palgrave Macmillan.

Bozeman, D P, Perrewe, P L, Kacmar, K M, Hochwarter, W A and Brymer, R A (1996) An examination of reactions to perceptions of organizational politics. Paper presented at the Southern Management Association Meeting, New Orleans, LA.

Bramley, P (2003) *Evaluating Training: From Personal Insight to Organisational Performance*, 2nd edn. London: Chartered Institute of Personnel and Development.

Brewington, J O and Nassar-McMillan, S (2000) 'Older adults: work-related issues and implications for counselling', *The Career Development Quarterly*, 49: 2–15.

Briscoe, J P, Hall, D T and Frautschy DeMuth, R L (2006) Protean and boundaryless careers: an empirical exploration, *Journal of Vocational Behavior*, 69: 30–47.

Burke, R (1993) Organizational level interventions to reduce occupational stress, *Work and Stress*, 7: 77–87.

Burtless, G (2013) The impact of population aging and delayed retirement on workforce productivity. Available at www.brookings.edu/research/papers/2013/05/impacting-aging-population-workforce-productivity (accessed 26 August 2015).

Business in the Community (2015) Business in the Community's Race into Work – Revisited. Available at http://raceforopportunity.bitc.org.uk/research-insight/research-articles/business-communitys-race-work-revisited and (accessed 1 October 2015).

Cadman, E (2015) Employers tap 'gig' economy in search of freelancers, *Financial Times*, 15 September. Available at www.ft.com/cms/s/0/ee293af0-5ab7-11e5-9846-de406ccb37f2.html#axzz3nJp7Zgmf (accessed 1 October 2015).

Cappelli, P (2001) *People Management*, 25 January, pp 38–40.

CBI (2009) Future fit: preparing graduates for the world of work. Available at www.cbi.org.uk/media/1121435/cbi_uuk_future_fit.pdf (accessed 20 August 2015).

Cerdin, J-L and Bird, A (2008) Careers in a global context, in Harris, M. (ed.), *Handbook of Research in International Human Resource Management* (pp 207–227). Mahwah, NJ: Lawrence Erlbaum.

Chang, C L-H, Chen, V, Klein, G and Jiang, J J (2011) Information system personnel career anchor changes leading to career changes, *European Journal of Information Systems*, 20: 103–117.

Chara, R (2010) Banking on talent, *People Management*, 28 October, pp 2–3.

Charan, R, Drotter, S and Noel, J (2011) *Leadership Pipeline: How to Build the Leadership Powered Company*. San Francisco, CA: Jossey-Bass.

Chen, H C and Naquin, S S (2006) An integrative model of competency development, training, assessment center and multi-rate assessment, *Advances in Developing Human Resources*, 8: 265–282.

Chen, J (2010) The influence of organizational socialisation tactics and information seeking on newcomer adjustment: evidence from two studies in China. Unpublished PhD thesis, University of Manchester.

CIPD (2012) Learning and Development Annual Survey Report 2012. Available at www.cipd.co.uk/binaries/5688%20LTD%20SR%20report%20WEB.pdf (accessed 23 September 2012).

CIPD (2015a) Learning and Development Annual Survey Report 2015. Available at www.cipd.co.uk/hr-resources/survey-reports/learning-development-2015.aspx (accessed 12 October 2015).

CIPD (2015b) Over-qualification and skills mismatch in the graduate labour market. Available at https://owa-legacy.uwe.ac.uk/owa/?ae=Item&a=Open&t=IPM.Note&id=RgAAAAB8%2f9gV9jg3T40z62Tx4bS1BwDyR%2fZ0iWviQ62CY8UoDivbAAAABXUXbAAA2HWsaK20ZQIGVXpR3JU PyAKQIppPubAAAJ (accessed 19 August 2015).

Clance, P R and Imes, S A (1978) The impostor phenomenon in high-achieving women: dynamics and therapeutic intervention, *Psychotherapy: Theory, Research and Practice*, 15(3).

Connor, H and Shaw, S (2008) Graduate training and development: current trends and issues, *Education and Training*, 50(5): 357–365.

Cooper-Thomas, H D and Burke, S E (2012) Newcomer proactive behavior: can there be too much of a good thing? In C. Wanberg (ed.), *Oxford Handbook of Organizational Socialization* (pp 56–77). New York, Oxford University Press.

Cornelius, N, Gooch, L and Todd, S (2001) Managing difference fairly: an integrated partnership approach. In Noon, M and Ogbonna, E (eds), *Equality, Diversity, and Disadvantage in Employment* (pp 32–50). Basingstoke: Palgrave.

Coutu, D L (2002) How resilience works, *Harvard Business Review*, May, 46–55.

Crawley, H (1996) Building a career portfolio in general practice, *BMJ*, 313: S2–7065, Available at www.bmj.com/content/313/7065/S2-7065 (accessed 20 February 2016).

Crumpacker, M and Crumpacker, J D (2007) Succession planning and generational differences: should HR consider age-based values and attitudes a relevant factor or a passing fad? *Public Personnel Management*, 36(4): 349–369.

Crush, P (2013) Five things HR gets wrong with appraisals. Available at www.cipd.co.uk/pm/peoplemanagement/b/weblog/archive/2013/04/05/five-things-hr-gets-wrong-with-appraisals.aspx (accessed 20 August 2015).

Csikszentmihalyi, M and Csikszentmihalyi, I S (eds) (1988) *Optimal Experience*. Cambridge: Cambridge University Press.

Cuddy, A C and Fiske, S T (2002) Doddering but dear: process, content, and functioning in stereotyping of older persons. In Nelson, T (ed.), *Ageism: Stereotyping and Prejudice Against Older Persons*, pp 1–26. Cambridge, MA: MIT Press.

Cullinane, N and Dundon, T (2006) The psychological contract: a critical review, *International Journal of Management Reviews*, 8(2): 113–129.

De Grip, A, Loo, J and Sanders, J (2004) The industry employability index: taking account of supply and demand characteristics, *International Labour Review*, 143(3).

Deal, T E and Kennedy, A A (1982) *Corporate Cultures: The Rites and Rituals of Corporate Life*. Harmondsworth: Penguin.

Department for Business Innovation and Skills (2015) Women on boards numbers almost doubled in last 4 years. Available at www.gov.uk/government/news/women-on-boards-numbers-almost-doubled-in-last-4-years (accessed 25 August 2015).

Department of Health (2015) Culture change in the NHS: applying the lessons of the Francis Inquiries. Available at www.gov.uk/government/uploads/system/uploads/attachment_data/file/403010/culture-change-nhs.pdf (accessed 31 August 2015).

Dipboye, R L (1995) How organizational politics can destructure human resource management in the interest of empowerment, support, and justice. In Cropanzano, R and Kacmar, M (eds), *Organizational Politics, Justice and Support* (pp 55–82). Westport, CT: Quorum Books.

Dries, N, Pepermans, R and De Kerpel, E (2008) Exploring four generations beliefs about careers: is 'satisfied' the new 'successful'? *Journal of Managerial Psychology*, 23(8): 907–928.

Drory, A and Beaty, D (1991) Gender differences in the perception of organizational influence tactics, *Journal of Organizational Behavior*, 12: 249–258.

Drory, A and Vigoda-Gadot, E (2010) Organizational politics and human resource management: a typology and the Israeli experience, *Human Resource Management Review*, 20: 194–202.

Dunkley, E (2015) Lloyds forced to put aside further £500m for PPI mis-selling, *Financial Times*, 28 October. Available at www.ft.com/cms/s/0/20db83e0-7d45-11e5-a1fe-567b37f80b64.html#axzz40jIg6QF0 (accessed 20 February 2016).

Dychtwald, K, Erickson, T and Morison, B (2006) It's time to retire retirement, *Harvard Business Review*, March, pp 48–58.

Easton, M (2014) Vicar or publican – which jobs make you happy? Available at www.bbc.co.uk/news/magazine-26671221 (accessed 22 February 2016).

Eisner, S P (2005) Managing generation Y, *Advanced Management Journal*, 70: 4–12.

El-Sawad, A, Arnold, J and Cohen, L (2004) 'Doublethink': the prevalence and function of contradiction in accounts of organisational life, *Human Relations*, 57(9): 1179–1203.

Employment Tribunals Service (2010) Employment tribunal and employment appeal tribunal statistics (GB) 1 April 2009 to 31 March, 2010. Available at www.employmenttribunals.gov.uk/news.htm (accessed 4 July 2010).

Equality and Human Rights Commission (2010) How fair is Britain? The first Triennial Review, Equality and Human Rights Commission. Available at www.equalityhumanrights.com/about-us/our-work/key-projects/how-fair-britain (accessed 1 December 2015).

European Parliament (2003) Directive 2003/88/EC of the European Parliament and of the Council of 4 November 2003 concerning certain aspects of the organisation of working time. Available at http://eur-lex.europa.eu/legal-content/EN/TXT/?uri=uriserv:OJ.L_.2003.299.01.0009.01.ENG (accessed 6 February 2016**).**

Feldman, D C (1976) A contingency theory of socialization, *Administrative Science Quarterly*, 21: 433–452.

Feldman, D C (1981) The multiple socialization of organization members, *Academy of Management Review*, 6: 309–318.

Ference, T P, Stoner, J A F and Warren, E K (1977) Managing the career plateau, *Academy of Management Review*, 2: 602–612.

Ferris, G R and King, T R (1991) Politics in human resources decisions: a walk on the dark side, *Organizational Dynamics*, 20: 59–71.

Fisher, C and Lovell, A (2009) *Business Ethics and Business Values*. Harlow: Prentice Hall.

Francis, R (2013) *Report of the Mid Staffordshire NHS Foundation Trust Public Inquiry*. Norwich: The Stationery Office.

Freudenberger, H (1974) Staff burnout, *Journal of Social Issues*, 30: 159–164.

Friedman, A L (2012) *Continuing Professional Development*. London: Routledge.

Fugate, M and Kinicki, A J (2008) A dispositional approach to employability: development of a measure and test of implications for employee reactions to organizational change, *Journal of Occupational and Organizational Psychology*, 81(3) 503–527.

Furnham, A (2015) Telling someone they are talented is disastrous, *People Management*, November, pp 44–45.

Gandz, J and Murray, V (1980) The experience of workplace politics, *Academy of Management Journal*, 23(2): 237–251.

Giannantonio, C M and Hurley-Hanson, A (2006) Applying image norms across super's career development stages, *The Career Development Quarterly*, 54(4): 318–330.

Gibson, D E and Barron, L A (2003) 'Exploring the impact of role models on older employees', *Career Development International*, 8: 198–210.

Gold, J and Smith, J (2010) Continuing professional development and life-long learning, in Gold, J, Holden, R, Iles, P, Stewart, J and Beardwell, J (eds), *Human Resource Development Theory and Practice*. Basingstoke: Palgrave Macmillan.

Goleman, D (1998) *Working with Emotional Intelligence*. London: Bloomsbury.

Guest, D (1998) Is the psychological contract worth taking seriously? *Journal of Organizational Behaviour*, 19: 649–664.

Guest, D (2004) The psychology of the employment relationship: an analysis based on the psychological contract, *Applied Psychology*, 53: 541–555.

Gutridge, M, Komm, A B and Lawson, E (2006) The people problem in talent management, *The McKinsey Quarterly Review*, 76: 137–152.

Hall, D T (1976) *Careers in Organisations*. Glenview, IL: Scott, Foresman.

Hall, D T (2002) *Careers In and Out of Organisations*. Thousand Oaks, CA: Sage.

Hall, D T and Associates (1996) *The Career is Dead—Long Live the Career: A Relational Approach to Careers*. San Francisco, CA: Jossey-Bass.

Hall, E T (1977) *Beyond Culture*. New York: Anchor.

Hamel, G and Valikangas, L (2003) The quest for resilience, *Harvard Business Review*, September, pp 52–63.

Hamori, M and Koyuncu, B (2013) The CEO experience trap, *MIT Sloan Management Review Magazine*, 12 September, p 14.

Handy, C (1991) *The Age of Unreason*. London: Century Press.

Handy, C (1994a) *The Empty Raincoat: Making Sense of the Future*. London: Hutchinson.

Handy, C (1994b) *The Age of Paradox*. Boston, MA: Harvard Business School Press.

Handy, C (2002) What's business for? *Harvard Business Review*, December, pp 49–55.

Hassard, J, Morris, J and McCann, L (2012) 'My brilliant career'? New organizational forms and changing managerial careers in Japan, the UK, and USA, *Journal of Management Studies*, 49(3): 571–599.

Hayman, K and Lorman, A (2004) Graduate training schemes have demonstrably accelerated promotion patterns, *Career Development International*, 9(2): 123–141.

Heckscher, C (1995) *White Collar Blues: Management Loyalties in an Age of Corporate Restructuring*. New York: Basic Books.

Heneman, R (1992) *Merit Pay: Linking Pay Increases and Performance Ratings*. Reading, MA: Addison-Watley.

Higher Education Statistics Agency (HESA) (2014a) Which subjects have the best employment prospects? Available at www.hesa.ac.uk/index.php?option=com_content&view=article&id=1899&Itemid=239 (accessed 7 August 2014).

Higher Education Statistics Agency (HESA) (2014b) HESA destinations of leavers survey 2012/13: what industries do employed leavers enter? Available at www.hesa.ac.uk/index.php?option=com_content&view=article&id=1899&Itemid=239 (accessed 7 August 2014).

Higher Education Statistics Agency (HESA) (2015) Qualifications obtained by level 2000/01 to 2013/14. Available at www.hesa.ac.uk/stats (accessed on 4 April 2015).

Hofstede, G (1984) *Culture's Consequences: International Differences in Work-Related Values*, 2nd edn. Beverly Hills CA: Sage.

Hogarth, T, Winterbotham, M, Hasluck, C, Carter, K, Daniel, W W, Green, A E and Morrison, J (2007) *Employer and University Engagement in the Use and Development of Graduate Skills*. London: Department for Education and Skills.

Holland, J L (1977) Manual for the vocational preference inventory. Palo Alto, CA: Consulting Psychologists Press.

Holland, J L (1997) Making vocational choices: a theory of vocational personalities and work environments, 3rd edn. Odessa, FL: Psychological Assessment Resources.

Honey, P (1986) The learning styles questionnaire. Available at www.peter honey.com/content/LearningStylesQuestionnaire.html (accessed 2 February 2016).

Honey, P and Mumford, A (1986) *The Manual of Learning Styles*, 2nd edn. Maidenhead: Peter Honey Publications.

Hughes, E C (1937) Institutional office and the person, *American Journal of Psychology*, 43: 404–413.

ICEF (2012) China and India to produce 40% of global graduates by 2020. Available at http://monitor.icef.com/2012/07/china-and-india-to-produce-40-of-global-graduates-by-2020/ (accessed 20 February 2016).

Inkson, K, Gunz, H, Ganesh, S and Roper, J (2012) Boundaryless careers: bringing back boundaries, *Organization Studies*, 33(3): 323–340.

International Labour Organization (2011) Equality at work: the continuing challenge. Paper presented at the International Labour Conference, 100th Session. Available at www.ilo.org/wcmsp5/groups/public/---ed_norm/---declaration/documents/publication/wcms_166583.pdf (accessed 29 May 2015).

Jablin, F M (2001) Organizational entry, assimilation and disengagement/exit. In Jablin, F M and Putnam, L L (eds), *New Handbook of Organizational Communication: Advances in Theory, Research and Methods* (pp 732–818). Thousand Oaks, CA: Sage.

Janis, I L (1971) Groupthink, *Psychology Today*, 5(6): 43–46, 74–76.

Johnson, J A and Lopes, J (2008) The intergenerational workforce revisited, *Organisation Development Journal*, 26(1): 31–36.

Jurkiewicz, C L (2000) Generation X and the public employee, *Public Personnel Management*, 29: 55–74.

Kanter, R M (1977) *Men and Women of the Corporation*. New York: Basic Books.

Keynes, J M (1930 [1963]) Economic possibilities for our grandchildren. In Keynes, J M (ed.), *Essays in Persuasion*, pp 358–373. New York: Norton.

Kimenyi, M S (2015) Leapfrogging traditional service delivery constraints in Africa through mobile technologies. Available at www.brookings.edu/blogs/africa-in-focus/posts/2015/03/11-leapfrogging-africa-mobile-technologies-kimenyi (accessed 14 August 2015).

Kirton, H (2015) Appraisals are finished. What next? Available at www.cipd.co.uk/pm/peoplemanagement/b/weblog/archive/2015/08/20/appraisals-are-finished-what-next.aspx (accessed 9 February 2016).

Knight, M and Yorke, P T (2003) *Embedding Employability into the Curriculum*. York: Higher Education Academy.

Knocke, J S (2015) Repatriation of international assignees – a systematic literature review from 1991 to 2014, Academy of Management Proceedings, January.

Available at http://proceedings.aom.org/content/2015/1/11050.short?related-urls=yes&legid=amproc;2015/1/11050 (accessed 9 November 2015).

Kotter, J P (1995) Why transformation efforts fail, *Harvard Business Review*, 85(1): 96–103.

Kroft, K, Lange, F and Notowidigdo, M J (2012) Duration dependence and labor market conditions: theory and evidence from a field experiment, NBER Working Paper No. 18387. Cambridge, MA: National Bureau of Economic Research.

Krosnick, J A and Alwin, D F (1989) Aging and susceptibility to attitude change, *Journal of Personality and Social Psychology*, 57(3): 416–425.

Kübler-Ross, E (1969) *On Death and Dying*. New York: Scribner.

Lawrence, B.S. (1988) 'New wrinkles in the theory of age: demography, norms and performance ratings', *Academy of Management Journal*, 31: 309–337.

Lazarova, M, Cerdin, J-L and Liao, Y (2014) The internationalism career anchor: a validation study, *International Studies of Management and Organisation*, 44(2): 9–33.

Levinson, D L with Darrow, C N, Klein, E B, Levinson, M H and McKee, B (1978) *The Seasons of a Man's Life*. New York: Knopf.

Levy, B (1996) Improving memory in old age through implicit self-stereotyping, *Journal of Personality & Social Psychology*, 71: 1092–1107.

Levy, B R and Langer, E (1994) Aging free from negative stereotypes: successful memory in China and among the American deaf, *Journal of Personality and Social Psychology*, 66: 989–997.

Louis, M R (1980) Surprise and sense making: what newcomers experience in entering unfamiliar organizational settings, *Administrative Science Quarterly*, 25: 226–251.

Lowry, D (2006) HR Managers as ethical decision makers: mapping the terrain, Asia *Pacific Journal of Human Resources*, 44(2): 171–183.

Luthans, F (2002) The need for and meaning of positive organizational behavior, *Journal of Organizational Behavior*, 23(6): 695–706.

Lyons, S T, Ng, E S and Schweitzer, L (2014) Launching a career: inter-generational differences in early career stages based on retrospective accounts. In Parry, E (ed.), *Generational Diversity at Work* (pp 149–163). Abingdon: Routledge.

Mandilaras, A (2004) Industrial placement and degree performance: evidence from a British higher institution, *International Review of Economics Education*, 3(1): 39–51.

Marquardt, M and Banks, S (2010) Theory to practice: action learning, *Advances in Developing Human Resources*, 12(2): 159–162.

Marsh, R M and Mannari, H (1997) Organizational commitment and turnover – a predictive study, *Administrative Science Quarterly*, 22: 57–75.

Marton, F and Ramsden, P (1988) What does it take to improve learning? In Ramsden, P (ed.), *Improving Learning*. London: Kogan Page.

Maslach, C (1986) Stress, burnout and workaholism. In Killberg, R R, Nathan, P E, Thoreson, R W (eds), *Professionals in Distress: Issues Syndromes and Solutions in Psychology*, pp 53–73. Washington, DC: American Psychological Association.

Maslach, C (1993) Burnout: a multidimensional perspective. In Schaufeli, W B, Maslach, C and Marek, T (eds), *Professional Burnout: Recent Developments in Theory and Research*. Washington, DC: Taylor and Francis.

Mayer, J D and Salovey, P (1997) What is emotional intelligence? In Salovey, P and Sluyter, D (eds), *Emotional Development and Emotional Intelligence: Educational Implications* (pp 3–31). NewYork: Basic Books.

McCann, R and Giles, H (2002) Ageism in the workplace: a communication perspective. In Nelson, T (ed.), *Ageism, Stereotyping, and Prejudice Towards Older People* (pp 163–20). Cambridge, MA: MIT Press.

McDermott, E, Mangan, J and O'Connor, M (2006) Graduate development programmes and satisfaction levels, *Journal of European Industrial Training*, 30(6): 456–471.

Mendez, R and Rona, A (2010) The relationship between industrial placements and final degree results: a study of engineering placement students, *Learning and Teaching in Higher Education*, 4(2): 46–61.

Meyer, J P and Allen, N J (1997) *Commitment in the Workplace: Theory, Research, and Application*. Thousand Oaks, CA: Sage.

Ministry of Justice (2012) Employment Tribunals and EAT Statistics, 2011–12: 1 April 2011 to 31 March 2012. Available at www.gov.uk/government/ uploads/system/uploads/attachment_data/file/218497/employment-trib-stats-april-march-2011-12.pdf (accessed 29.2.16).

Moltke, H G von, (1900) *Militärische Werke*, vol. 2, part 2, pp 33–40. Berlin: Mittler.

Moorhead, G and Griffin, R W (1989) *Organizational Behaviour*. Boston, MA: Houghton Mifflin.

Morrison, E W (1993) Newcomer information seeking: exploring types, modes, sources and outcomes, *Academy of Management Journal*, 36: 557–589.

Myers & Briggs Foundation (2014) Personality and careers. Available at www.myersbriggs.org/type-use-for-everyday-life/personality-and-careers/ (accessed 4 October 2015).

Myers & Briggs Foundation (2015) MBTI® basics. Available at www.myers briggs.org/my-mbti-personality-type/mbti-basics/ (accessed 1 November 2015).

Nadler, L and Wiggs, G D (1986) *Managing Human Resource Development*. San Francisco, CA: Jossey-Bass.

Neugebauer, J and Evans-Brain, J (2009) *Making the Most of Your Placement*. London: Sage.

Newell, S and Shackleton, V (2001) Selection and assessment as an interactive decision process. In Redman, T and Wilkinson, A (eds), *Contemporary Human Resource Management*, pp 24–56. London: Prentice Hall.

Noon, M (2007) The fatal flaws of diversity and the business case for ethnic minorities, *Work Employment and Society*, 21(4): 773–784.

Northouse, P G (2007) *Leadership: Theory and Practice*. Thousand Oaks, CA: Sage.

O'Donnell, H, Karallis, T, Sandelands, E, Cassin, J and O'Neill, D (2008) Case study: developing graduate engineers at Kentz Engineers and Constructors, *Education and Training*, 50(5): 439–452.

Oates, W (1971) *Confessions of a Workaholic: The Facts about Addiction*. New York: World.

OECD (2012) Education indicators in focus. Available at www.oecd.org/edu/50495363.pdf (accessed 14 August 2015).

OECD (2013) Average annual working time: hours per worker. Available at www.oecd-ilibrary.org/employment/average-annual-working-time_20752342-table8 (accessed 26 August 2015).

OECD (2015) Skills outlook 2015: first results from the survey of adult skills. Available at www.oecd.org/education/oecd-skills-outlook-2015–978926 4234178-en.htmOECD (accessed 28 May 2015).

ONS (2013) Pension trends – Chapter 4: the labour market and retirement, 2013 edition. Available at 2015www.ons.gov.uk/ons/dcp171766_297899.pdf (accessed 26 August 2015).

ONS (2014) Sickness Absence in the labour market, 2014. Available at www.ons.gov.uk/ons/publications/re-reference-tables.html?edition=tcm%3A 77-351500 (accessed 19 August 2015).

ONS (2015a) The latest on the labour market. Available at www.ons.gov.uk/ons/rel/lms/labour-market-statistics/march-2015/sty-labour-market-statistics--march (accessed 18 March 2015).

ONS (2015b) International comparisons of productivity: final estimates for 2013. Available at www.ons.gov.uk/ons/rel/icp/international-comparisons-of-productivity/2013---final-estimates/info-icp-feb-15.html (accessed 26 August 2015).

Osland, J and Bird, A (2000) Beyond sophisticated stereotyping: cultural sensemaking in context, *Academy of Management Executive*, 14(1): 65–79.

Parry, E (ed.) (2014) *Generational Diversity at Work*. Abingdon: Routledge.

Parry, E, Unite, J, Chudzikowski, K, Briscoe, J P and Shen, Y (2012) Career success in the younger generation. In Ng, E, Lyons, S and Schweitzero L (eds), *Managing the New Workforce: International Perspectives on the Millennial Generation* (pp 242–261). Cheltenham: Edward Elgar.

Pathiraja, F and Wilson, M-C (2011) The rise and rise of the portfolio career, BMJ Careers. Available at http://careers.bmj.com/careers/advice/view-article.html?id=20001807 (accessed 20 February 2016).

Pegg, A, Waldock, J, Hendy-Isaac, S and Lawton, R (2012) Pedagogy for employability. Available at www.heacademy.ac.uk/assets/documents/employability/pedagogy_for_employability_update_2012.pdf (accessed 17 June 2015).

Pettigrew, T F (1998) Intergroup contact theory, *Annual Review of Psychology*, 47: 65–85.

Pilbeam, S and Corbridge, M (2006) *People Resourcing: Contemporary HRM in Practice*, 3rd edn. Harlow: Prentice Hall.

Rajan, A, Van Eupen, P, Chapple, K and Lane, D (2000) Employability: bridging the gap between rhetoric and reality, first report: employer's perspective. London: Create Consultancy/Professional Development Foundation.

Raybould, J and Sheedy, V (2005) Are graduates equipped with the right skills in the employability stakes? *Industrial and Commercial Training*, 37(5): 259–263.

Rees, B (2003) *The Construction of Management: Gender Issues and Competence Techniques in Modern Organisations*. Cheltenham: Edward Elgar.

Rhodes, S R (1983) Age-related differences in work attitudes and behavior: a review and conceptual analysis, *Psychological Bulletin*, 93: 328–367.

Rivera, L (2015) *Pedigree: How Elite Students Get Elite Jobs*. Princeton, NJ: Princeton University Press.

Roberts, G (1997) *Recruitment and Selection: A Competency Approach*. London: Institute of Personnel and Development.

Rokeach, M (1973) *The Nature of Human Values*. New York: The Free Press.

Romanowska, J (1993) Employee development through education liaison, *Education and Training*, 35(3): 58–71.

Rose, Lord (2015) Better leadership for tomorrow: NHS Leadership Review. London: Department of Health.

Rothwell, A and Arnold, J (2007) Self-perceived employability: development and validation of a scale, *Personnel Review*, 36(1): 23–41.

Rousseau, D (1989) Psychological and implicit contracts in organisations, *Employee Responsibilities and Rights Journal*, 2: 121–139.

Rousseau, D (1990) New hire perceptions of their own and employers' obligations: a study of psychological contracts, *Journal of Organizational Behavior*, 11: 389–400.

Rousseau, D (1995) *Psychological Contracts in Organisations*. Thousand Oaks, CA: Sage.

Rousseau, D and Greller M (1994) Human resource practices: administrative contract makers, *Human Resources Management*, 33(3): 385–401.

Rowley, J (2014) Degree deceit: does it pay to lie on your CV? *The Guardian*, 18 June. Available at www.theguardian.com/careers/careers-blog/lie-degree-cv-jobseekers-graduate accessed 9 February 2016).

Sala, F, Mount, G J and Druskat, V U (eds) (2005) *Linking Emotional Intelligence and Performance at Work: Current Research Evidence with Individuals and* Group. Mahwah, NJ: Lawrence Erlbaum.

Salisbury, J D (2006) Organizational socialization of adjunct faculty members at Baker College: a correlational analysis of content, context, and the dimensions that affect socialization outcomes. Unpublished PhD thesis, Capella University, Minneapolis.

Sands, N (2010) Fantasist Stephen Wilce leaves New Zealand military red-faced. Available at www.news.com.au/world/fantasist-stephen-wilce-leaves-new-zealand-military-red-faced/story-e6frfkyi-1225944975775 (accessed 24 March 2016).

Schaufeli, W B, Salanova, M, Gonzalez-Roma, V and Bakker, A B (2002) The measurement of engagement and burnout: a two sample confirmatory factor analysis and approach, *Journal of Happiness Studies*, 3: 71–92.

Schaufeli, W B, Taris, T W and van Rhenen, W (2008) Workaholism, burnout, and work engagement: three of a kind or three different kinds of employee well being? *Applied Psychology: An International Review*, 57(2): 173–203.

Schein, E H (1970) *Organizational Psychology*. Englewood Cliffs, NJ: Prentice-Hall.

Schein, E H (1990) *Career Anchors: Discovering Your Real Values*. San Diego, CA: Pfeiffer.

Schein, E H (1999) *The Corporate Survival Guide*. San Francisco, CA: Jossey-Bass.

Schumpeter (2015) Not-so-happy returns: big businesses fail to make the most of employees with foreign experience, *The Economist*, 7 November. Available at www.economist.com/news/business/21677634-big-businesses-fail-make-most-employees-foreign-experience-not-so-happy-returns (accessed 10 February 2016).

Seneca, L A (5BC–65AD [1997]) *On the Shortness of Life* (Costa, C D N, trans. and ed.). London: Penguin.

Senge, P M (1990) *The Fifth Discipline: The Art and Practice of the Learning Organization*. London: Random House.

Sissons, P (2011) The hourglass and the escalator: labour market change and mobility, The Work Foundation. Available at www.theworkfoundation. com/downloadpublication/report/292_hourglass_escalator120711%20 (2)%20(3).pdf (accessed 14 August 2015).

Smola, K W and Sutton, C D (2002) Generational differences: revisiting generational work values for the new millennium, *Journal of Organizational Behavior*, 23: 363–382.

Social Mobility and Child Poverty Commission (2015) A qualitative evaluation of non-educational barriers to the elite professions. Available at www.gov. uk/government/uploads/system/uploads/attachment_data/file/434791/ A_qualitative_evaluation_of_non-educational_barriers_to_the_elite_ professions.pdf (accessed 14 June 2015).

Sparrow, P R (1996) Careers and the psychological contract: understanding the European context, *European Journal of Work and Organizational Psychology*, 5(4): 479–500.

Steele, C M and Aranson, J (1995) Stereotype threat and intellectual test performance of African Americans, *Journal of Personality and Social Psychology*, 69: 797–811.

Stone, D and Heen, S (2014) *Thanks for the Feedback: The Science and Art of Receiving Feedback Well*. New York: Penguin.

Storey, J and Sisson, K (1993) *Managing Human Resources and Industrial Relations*. Buckingham: The Open University Press.

Suff, R (2010) Benchmarking competencies: the 2010 survey, *IRS Employment Review*, 23 August.

Super, D E (1957) *The Psychology of Careers*. New York: Harper and Row.

Suutari, V and Taka, M (2004) Career anchors of managers with global careers, *Journal of Management Development*, 23(9): 833–847.

Tan, C S and Salamone, P R (1994) 'Understanding career plateauing: implications for counseling', *The Career Development Quarterly*, 42(4): 291.

Tempest, S, McKinlay, A and Starkey, K (2004) Careering alone: careers and social capital in the financial services and television industries, *Human Relations*, 57(12): 1523–1545.

The Guardian (2015) Swedish fathers to get third month of paid paternity leave, 28 May. Available at www.theguardian.com/world/2015/may/28/ swedish-fathers-paid-paternity-parental-leave (accessed 25 August 2015).

Tolman, C W, Cherry, F, van Hezewijk, R and Lubek, I (eds) (1996) *Problems of Theoretical Psychology – ISTP 1995*. Belfast: Captus University Publications.

Tuckman, B (1965) Developmental sequence in small groups, *Psychological Bulletin*, 63(6): 384–399.

UK Government (2015) Whistleblowing for employees. Available at www.gov. uk/whistleblowing/what-is-a-whistleblower (accessed 10 February 2016).

United Nations (UN) (2015) World population prospects: the 2015 revision. Available at http://esa.un.org/unpd/wpp/Publications/Files/Key_Findings_WPP_2015.pdf (accessed 14 August 2015).

UWE (2012) Mobile phone runs on urine power. Available at https://info.uwe.ac.uk/news/uwenews/news.aspx?id=259 (accessed 14 August 2015).

Van der Heijden, B (2002) Prerequisites to guarantee life-long employability, *Personnel Review*, 31(1): 44–61.

Van Wanrooy, B, Bewley, H, Bryson, A, Forth, J, Freeth, S, Stokes, L and Wood, S (2013) The 2011 Workplace Employment Relations Study: first findings. Available at https://www.gov.uk/government/uploads/system/uploads/attachment_data/file/336651/bis-14-1008-WERS-first-findings-report-fourth-edition-july-2014.pdf (accessed 2 February 2016).

Wall Street Journal (2015) Japan has plenty of jobs but workers still struggle. Available at www.wsj.com/articles/japan-has-plenty-of-jobs-but-workers-still-struggle-1426197511 (accessed 14 August 2015).

Whiddet, S and Hollyforde, S (2003) *A Practical Guide to Competences*. London: CIPD.

Wiese, D S and Buckley, R M (1998) The evolution of the performance appraisal process, *Journal of Management History*, 4(3): 233–249.

Wimer, S and Nowack, K M (1998) 13 Common Mistakes Using 360-degree Feedback, *Training and Development*, 52(5): 69–70.

Youssef, C M and Luthans, F (2007) Positive organizational behavior in the workplace: the impact of hope, optimism and resilience, *Journal of Management*, 33(5): 774–800.

Yu, H-C and Miller, P (2005) Leadership style: the X Generation and Baby Boomers compared in different cultural contexts, *Leadership and Organization Development Journal*, 26(1).

Index

NOTE: page numbers in *italic type* refer to tables.